Ultimate Money Guide to
NFT INVESTING 2021

Non-Fungible Token (NFT) for Beginners

Step by step guide to trading and investing
in NFT Crypto

Legal Disclaimer:

Please note that the information in this book is for educational and informational purposes only. Technology, Business, Medicine, and other topics in this book are always changing. The purpose of this book is to provide information with currently available knowledge and understanding based on the author's best efforts at that time without any kind, express, or implied warranty. It is NOT intended to be used as a substitute for any advice (including but not limited to) Legal, Technology, investing, and Medical, or any other services.

Readers should use their judgment and own advisors for all decisions and should not base or rely on this book for any decisions. We disclaim all warranties or implied warranties concerning all content on this book. Readers should consult their business professionals or licensed professional for any business and investing advice. Readers should consult an attorney for any legal advice.

The author(s) have made every effort to provide accurate, reliable, and up-to-date information, while due to the possibility of human errors or change/updates, author(s) do not guarantee that all information included is complete or accurate, and disclaim all responsibilities for any omissions or error, or the results obtained from using the information contained in this document.

Author(s) has no obligation to warrant the accuracy or appropriateness of any third-party websites or URLs. The listing of any person, business, hyperlinks, or others in this book does not constitute an endorsement or recommendation by the author(s). If a reader chooses to click on links and be taken to an external website belonging to a third party, then the reader and only the reader shall be responsible and liable for his/her actions should you suffer or incur any harm or loss from the usage of such information. Some of the links are affiliate links, which means if you click on the link and purchase the item, the author(s) will receive an affiliate commission. This commission may be in the form of money, services, or complimentary products and could exist without any action from the website visitor. These will not cost you anything, but it helps the author(s) offset the costs.

By reading this, the reader agrees that under no circumstances is the author(s) responsible for any direct or indirect losses incurred due to using this document's information, including not limited to omissions, inaccuracies, or errors. You agree to hold the author(s) harmless from ALL (including but not limited to) claims, losses, damages, etc.

Table of Contents

Introduction

Chapter 1 Blockchain, Cryptocurrency, and NFT

1.1 To Understand NFT, We Need To Know About Blockchain

1.2 How Blockchain Turn Into Cryptocurrency

1.3 Different Types Of Cryptocurrency

1.4 What is NFT

1.5 Why NFT

1.6 Why NFT Use Ethereum And Not Other Cryptocurrency

1.7 History Of NFT

1.8 Why are Non-Fungible Tokens in the Spotlight Recently?

1.9 How Big is the NFT market Now?

Chapter 2 NFT Value and Wallet

2.1 Understanding the Value of NFT and How to Increase Potential Value

2.2 Understanding Why Some NFTs are Selling for Millions of Dollars

2.3 Choosing Wallets to Get Started Investing NFTs

Chapter 3 Investing By Creating NFTs

3.1 Should You Create Your Own NFT Artworks?

3.2 Can Your Content Be an NFT?

3.3 What Needed to Start Creating NFTs? Step-by-Step Instructions

3.4 How to Create NFT Art With No Coding Experience

3.5 Why It Can Be Expensive To Create NFTs?

3.6 How To Create NFTs for Free without Gas Fees

3.7 Related Legal Issues Worth Your Attention

Chapter 4 Investing by Buying NFTs

4.1 What Do You Get When You Purchase NFTs?

4.2 What Makes an NFT original?

4.3 How Much Do You Need to Spend?

4.4 Where & How You Can Buy and Sell NFTs

4.5 How To Find Valuable NFTs

4.6 Which NFT Industries Worth Most Of Your Attention Now

4.7 What's the Disadvantage Of Trading NFTs

4.8 Are There Risks and Scams To Be Aware Of?

Chapter 5 NFT Selling, Trading & Swapping

5.1 As NFT Creators or Artists, How to Make Sales

5.2 As NFT collectors, How to Value NFTs

5.3 NFT Trading & Swapping

5.4 Environmental Impacts of NFT Trading

Chapter 6 Let's Delve Into NFT Use Cases

Chapter 7 Other Ways to Generate Revenue From NFT

7.1 NFT Lending & Borrowing

7.2 NFT Royalties

Chapter 8   Other Options to Get Exposures to NFTs

Chapter 9 NFT Risks and Scams & How to Avoid Them

9.1 NFT Major Trading Risks

9.2 NFT Scams You Must Avoid

Chapter 10 What's Next for NFTs?

Conclusion

References

Introduction

Recently, Twitter CEO Jack Dorsey made headlines selling the first-ever tweet as an NFT for $2.9 million. A 10-year-old meme, the animated GIF of Nyan Cat, was sold for more than $500,000. In March 2021, The "Everydays-The first 5000 Days NFT" from the digital artist- Beeple has been sold for an astonishing $69 million. Another of his NFT artwork-"Crossroads," was also sold for more than $66,666.66 in Feb.

Yes. You've probably heard about by now: non-fungible tokens, or NFT's for short. This new type of investment has taken the world by storm, turning digital artworks and collectibles into easily tradable items on the blockchain.

This is the $1 Trillion Opportunity you won't want to miss.

Currently, the global collectibles market alone is worth almost $400 billion. Fine wines, classic cars, comics books, and even film props have already earned places in collector museums and homes. Once you add all artworks ever produced in the total values, the figure likely tops $1 trillion.

Today, we are standing at the precipice of change. NFT market brings you the unique opportunity that you could start making money from things that were once untradable-digital music, art, and even your tweets on Twitter. Also, even the traditional world of physical art and collectibles is joining the NFT revolution.

This is a market you need to know.

However, what exactly are NFTs? How have those artists or organizations, including Grimes and NBA, created millions of dollars in sales? Of course, most importantly, how can regular investors, like you and me, get in early enough to make big profits?

The **Ultimate Money Guide to NFT Investing** covers almost everything you will need to know about blockchain technology, cryptocurrency, and NFTs, whether you are a digital artist, collector, trader, or investor.

You will learn:

- The basics of NFTs, blockchain, and cryptocurrency
- How to choose Crypto Wallets to get started investing NFTs
- How to **value** NFTs
- **Step-by-step** instructions on **creating** NFTs
- Everything that matters to you when you **buy** NFTs
- How to **Sell, Trade, and Swap** NFTs
- Other possible ways to **generate revenue** from NFTs
- Optional ways that you can **get exposed to NFTs** if you are not in the NFT ecosystem 24/7
- Major NFT **Investing risks and scams** that **you want to avoid**

... and More.

NFTs are creating exciting opportunities for all kinds of creators (musicians, visual arts, game designers, etc.) and unlocking new revenue streams. One of the most exciting parts is the variety of assets NFT can represent: digital artwork, virtual collectibles, game times, real estate, even tickets, certifications, identity documents, and many more. As the WAX co-founder, William E.Quigley, stated, "NFTs will stand side by side with music, video, games, and movies as a distinct format of entertainment. Every consumer product that cannot be eaten can become an NFT."

It would be such a pity to dismiss the NFT market because you don't understand it.

This handy guide provides you with key information and instructions that will help your NFT investment based on in-depth research. However, it is not just a theoretical presentation. You will learn practical knowledge with examples in the step-by-step and easy-to-understand approach. Even if you have little or no knowledge of NFTs, you will get confidence in this space too.

If you missed the cryptocurrencies train, then don't leave this opportunity on the table again!

Chapter 1

Blockchain, Cryptocurrency, and NFT

1.1 To Understand NFT, We Need To Know About Blockchain
What Is Blockchain?

Blockchain, sometimes also refers as Distributed Ledger Technology (DLT). It seems complex, and it definitely can be. However, its core concept is simple. Blockchain is a kind of database. But you may ask, what is a database?

A database is the information collection that is stored on the computer system electronically. The databases' data or information is typically structured in table format to search and filter for specific information easier.

A simple analogy is Google Doc. As we create a document and share it with other people, the document is distributed instead of transferred or copied. This will create a decentralized distribution chain giving everybody access to the document simultaneously. All modifications to the document are being recorded in real-time, and no one is locked out awaiting changes from other parties, which makes changes or modifications completely transparent.

What is the difference between using a Google Docs rather than a database to store information?

Google Docs is designed for one individual or small groups of people, and it is to access and store limited amounts of information. On the contrary, the database is designed to house significantly much more information that can be manipulated, filtered, and accessed easily and quickly by any number of users at the same time.

Servers made up of powerful computers are used for housing large databases. They can be composed of hundreds or even thousands of computers, which allows enough storage capacity and computational power for many users to access the large database at once.

Three critical ideas of the blockchain technologies:

- Digital assets are distributed rather than transferred or copied.
- The assets are decentralized and are allowed full real-time access.
- The integrity of the documents is preserved by the transparent ledger of changes, which creates the assets' trust.

How Does Blockchain Work?

Blockchain has three critical concepts: blocks, miners, and nodes.

- **Blocks**

Every chain is made of multiple blocks, and every block consists of three essential elements:

1) The **data** stored in the block.
2) Nonce. It's a 32-bit whole number and randomly generated when the block is created.
3) Hash. The hash is a 256-bit number and is generated when the nonce is created. It must start with a significant number of zeroes.

When the first block of the chain is created, a nonce generates the cryptographic hash. The block's data is also considered signed and tied to the nonce and hash forever unless it is mined.

- **Miners**

The process of generating new blocks on the chain is called mining. Every block in the blockchain has a unique nonce and hash and its own references of the previous block's hash in the chain, making mining a block difficult, especially on large chains.

The miners need to use the special software to solve the incredibly complicated math problems of discovering a nonce that can generate an accepted hash. Since the nonce is 32 bits and the hash is 256 bits, about four billion possible nonce-hash combinations have to be mined before the right one is found. That's when the miners announce that they find the "golden nonce," and their block is added to the chain.

If you make a change to any block earlier in the chain, it will require the re-mining of not just the modified block but all the blocks coming after. This is why manipulation blockchain is extremely difficult.

When a block is successfully mined, the modification will be accepted by all nodes on the network. The miner will also be financially rewarded.

- **Nodes**

The computers and any electronic devices that make up the blockchain's network are called nodes. One of the most crucial features of blockchain is decentralization. No organization or electronic device can own the chain. Instead, the nodes are considered the distributed ledger connected to the chain. In the blockchain, every node has a complete record of the data that has been stored on the blockchain since it's discovered.

Each node has its unique copy of the blockchain. The network will need to algorithmically approve any newly mined block to update and verify the chain. Blockchain is transparent; any actions in the ledger will be able to be viewed and checked. Every participant will be given a unique alphanumeric identification number showing their transaction.

If one node has an error within the data, it can use thousands of other nodes as the reference point to correct itself. This makes no single node within the network can modify information held within it.

1.2 How Blockchain Turn Into Cryptocurrency

Cryptocurrency is built upon blockchain technology. Because cryptocurrencies like Bitcoin were the first blockchain applications, many people may think they're interchangeable. However, in reality, cryptocurrencies are just one use case of blockchain technology.

The Federal Reserve controls the U.S. dollars. Under this central authority system, users' currency and data are technically at their governments or banks' whim. Let's say if a user's bank gets hacked, the client's private information will be at risk. Or if the clients live in a country with an unstable government or their banks collapse, their currency's value will be at risk. In 2008, some banks ran out of money and were bailed out partially by using taxpayers' money. This is how Bitcoins was first created and developed.

Blockchain allows cryptocurrencies to operate without the central authority by spreading their operations across the network of computers. Not only does this decrease the risk, but it eliminates many transaction or processing fees. Besides, it's able to provide those in countries with unstable financial infrastructures or volatile currencies a more stable version of money with a broader network of people and companies they can do business with.

Cryptocurrency has been brought to the general public's attention because of its speculative value. Quite a few people view them as investment opportunities, especially after the significant rise in Bitcoin prices last year.

However, there's an inherent issue in that speculation - coins' volatility. The $5,000 in coins can easily become $10,000 or $1,000 in a short time. This is the risk needed to take into account when investing in cryptocurrency. As more scams are involved, the SEC has stepped in. Cryptocurrency trading or investing is now under regulation by securities laws, like other non-crypto investments.

1.3 Different Types Of Cryptocurrency
Coins Vs. Crypto Tokens

Encrypted tokens and coins are both under the crypto. Generally, they can be categorized into two kinds of cryptocurrency: tokens and alternative cryptocurrency coins (Altcoins)

- **Tokens**

Tokens are created and distributed through the initial coin offering (ICO), similarly to stock offering. Tokens are represented as:

1) Utility tokens (for specific uses)
2) Value tokens (Bitcoins)
3) Security tokens (for protecting your accounts)

Actually, their primary function is not being used as money since they are designated for a function. Similarly to U.S. dollars, they represent the value, but not in themselves of value. Tokens cover many meanings, and they are one of the encryptions.

For example, Bitcoin and Ether (from Ehtereium) fall under the heading of tokens.

- **Alternative Cryptocurrency Coins (Also known as Altcoins)**

Basically, altcoins are any coins that are not Bitcoins. They include:

- Peercoin

- Dogecoin

- Litecoin

- Namecoin

- Auroracoin

Actually, the name "altcoin" refers to "alternative to Bitcoin." Among the above, the Namecoin is the first created altcoin, back in 2011.

Similar to Bitcoin, most cryptocurrencies mentioned here have a limited supply for reinforcing their perceived value and keeping the balance in check. For Bitcoin, only 21 million can exist, which was decided by the Bitcoin creator. The only way to generate more is by letting the coin's protocol allow for this.

Each coin's system can differ from the other, as they were created to serve different applications and purposes as well as identified differently.

The following cryptocurrencies don't work with the same open-source protocol as Bitcoin's and have created their own separate protocols and systems:

- Nxt
- Omni
- Ripple
- Ethereum
- Counterparty
- Waves

The Most Popular Types of Cryptocurrency (at present)

1. **Bitcoin (BTC)**

Bitcoin is possibly the "Coca-Cola" of all cryptocurrencies. It is the most closely associated with the cryptosystem and most recognizable. Currently, there are more than 18.5 million in circulation, against the present capped limit of 21 million.

2. **Litecoin (LTC)**

Litecoin is created in 2011 by Charlie Lee, a former Google employee, as an alternative to Bitcoin. Litecoin is believed to have lower fees, shorter transaction times, and more concentrated miners. The coin limit for LTC is 84 million.

Like BTC, LTC is with an open-source and completely decentralized global payment network.

3. **Bitcoin Cash**

Bitcoin cash was created in 2017 to improve certain features of Bitcoin. It's one of the most popular kinds of cryptocurrency on the market. Bitcoin cash has increased the blocks' size from 1 MB (of Bitcoin's) to 8 MB, allowing faster processing speeds and more transactions.

4. **Ethereum**

You can think of Ethereum as the app store since it focuses on decentralized applications - phone apps, rather than on digital currency. This platform takes away the control of apps from the middlemen like Apple and returns it to its original creators. So the only one who is able to make changes to the app is the original creator. Ether, which is the token used here, is the currency by app users and developers.

5. Stellar

Stellar is the intermediary currency and focuses on money transfers to facilitate money exchange. Jed McCaleb, the co-founder of Ripple, created it in 2014.

Stellar allows its users to send any currency they have to other people in a different currency. Its goal is to help develop economies that don't have access to investment opportunities and traditional banks. Users or institutions won't get charged by using its network, and the tax-deductible public donations they accepted can cover the operating costs.

6. Ripple

Ripple is not Blockchain-based and not for individual users. It majorly serves larger corporations and companies to move a larger amount of money globally.

Its popularity primarily got from its digital payment protocol, which allows transferring money in any form. Bitcoin can handle 3-6 transactions per second (tps), but Ripple can deal with 1,500 tps.

7. Cardano

It's claimed to be the only coin with a "research-driven approach and scientific philosophy.", which means it undergoes particularly rigorous reviews by programmers and scientists.

Cardano is used to send and receive digital funds and is considered to be a more sustainable and balanced ecosystem for crypto.

It's created by Charles Hoskinson, the co-founder of Ethereum.

8. NEO

NEO is previously known as Antshares and was created in China. Its main focus is smart or digital contracts that allow users to execute and create agreements without intermediaries. It's aggressively looking to become a major crypto player.

According to its creator Erik Zhang, it has three distinct advantages compared to its   major competitor-Ethereum:

- More developer-friendly digital contracts
- Better Architecture
- Easier integration of digital assets and identities into the real world

9. **IOTA**

IOTA stands for Internet of Things Application and was launched in 2016. Rather than working with blocks and chains like other blockchain technologies, it works with smart devices on the Internet of Things (IoT).

The Tangle used by IOTA needs devices to be capable of purchasing more bandwidth, electricity, data, or storage when they need them and sell these resources when they don't.

1.4 What is NFT

There are two types of tokens: Fungible Token (FT) and Non-Fungible Token (NFT).

For FTs, their main feature is that they are divisible and interchangeable. Popular FTs include Ethereum, Bitcoin, and Cortex.

For NFTs, they include something unique, so they're not replicable. The unique part is written inside the token's metadata and considered permanent and with an unalterable authenticity certificate. They're particularly useful as the ownership or proof of asset.

NFT can tokenize almost everything, the most common use cases (so far) include:

- Digital Art and Music
- Virtual Assets and addresses
- Gaming items (rare weapons and kins)
- Collectibles
- Tokenized luxury goods (e.g., wine)
- Real-world assets (ownership)

Let's talk about a few examples:

Digital Art and Music:

Mostly, the physical artworks are with more collectible value. If you purchase the artwork from a formal resource, you will get a guarantee with a laser label and a steel seal for sure. Nowadays, digital fingerprints for art are becoming popular. The commonly used anti-counterfeiting encryption technology is called art micro-jet. As the art micro-jet canvas is created, the anti-counterfeiting mark is embedded. This mark cannot be reproduced and cannot be seen by naked eyes. It requires scanned and verified by a dedicated App.

Tokenized Luxury Goods:

Let's use wine as an example, so what's good to tokenize the wine? Making the bottle of wine's process will be recorded through the IoT device, from grape harvesting, brewing, packaging to delivery. Since the information stored in blockchains is hard to tamper with, the wine's authenticity can be reviewed and certified. All information about this wine can be recorded and tracked, including whether the wine is from a specific winery or the grapes' source has been contaminated.

Collectibles

This is a huge market, including trading Jordan sneakers. With NFT, every collectible is unique, and the metadata the hold can be used to identify its authenticity.

1.5 Why NFT

Maybe you are wondering why do we need to use NFT and blockchain? Simply put, NFT can prevent fraud and forgery through traceable digital information like the assets' ownership recorded in the blockchain.

Three characteristics are making NFT the perfect tech for this work:

- **Easy to Trace**

The blockchain's data is transparent and open. It offers an innovative way to store patents, contracts, and other documents where users truly own their data, which is applied to NFT too. Anyone can check or view NFTs' ownership history, time of issuance, source, issuances' number, and much other information. Anything valuable can be tokenized by NFTs, building a connection between value and information.

- **Hard to Forge**

It's easy to replicate digital foodprints and hard for owners and creators to claim their digital rights. You can easily share pictures, music, and videos with others without actually owning them. It's also quite simple to forge a fake identity of the asset. With the help of NFT, artists and owners of digital assets can protect their artwork and prevent them from being forged. Since it's difficult to copy the artworks, it can better ensure the assets' value by guaranteeing their scarcity.

- **Increase Circulation**

Let's look at the gaming industry. In traditional gaming, the virtual treasure's value you bought is locked within the game company's server. If the company stops operating, you will lose the right to use the virtual treasure too. However, if it's made into NFT, you will be able to obtain the games' true ownership and freely trade them in the NFT auction market, which increases their circulation significantly.

More importantly, it only takes few minutes to finish the cross-border NFT transactions. The fraud's possibility will also be eliminated.

1.6 Why NFT Use Ethereum And Not Other Cryptocurrency

Currently, Ethereum is the most popular cryptocurrency to create NFTs. This is because NFTs are typically built with the ERC-721 token standard.

The ERC stands for "Ethereum Request for comment." The ERC-721 token is a term generally describing non-fungible tokens. If we break down this term, it refers to guiding standards as NFT creation atop the Etherium blockchain. So, NFT is a token kind built based on Ethereum's ERC-721 standard.

Besides Ehterum, NFTs can live on other decentralized networks, including NEO and EOS. However, it requires the platforms to have a box full of NFTs' tools and smart contract-capability that can enable detailed descriptions, like the metadata.

1.7 History Of NFT

2012-2013: Colored Coins

Colored coins are the smallest unit of a Bitcoin and are made of denominations of Bitcoins. No one could argue that they are the very first NFTs ever existed. Colored coins were used to represent assets' multitudes and have many use cases, such as:

- Access tokens
- Subscriptions
- Issue shares of a company
- Coupons
- Property
- Ability to issue your cryptocurrencies
- Digital collections

The flaws of the Colored Coins are apparent; they work best in a permissioned environment. Nonetheless, they laid much of the NFTs' groundwork and opened the door to NFT's further experimentation.

2014 – Counterparty

Although the colored coins' creation led people to realize the enormous potential for issuing assets using blockchain technology, people understood that Bitcoin was not meant to enable these extra features.

Adam Krellenstein, Even Wagner, and Robert Dermody then founded the Counterparty in 2014. It's a peer-to-peer financial platform with open-source Internet protocol atop Bitcoin's blockchains.

Counterparty allows decentralized-exchange assets' creation, as well as the crypto token with XCP ticket.

April 2015 – Counterparty, Spells of Genesis

The Spells of Genesis' game creators were the pioneers for using Counterparty to issue the in-game assets onto blockchains. Spells of Genesis founded development by producing the token named BitCrystals that's as the in-game currency.

August 2016- Counterparty, More Trading Cards

In August 2016, Counterparty collaborated with the popular trading card game - Force of Wil, the 4th ranked card game by sales in North America. They launched the trading cards on the Counterparty platform. The entrance of the game company into the ecosystem signaled the value of putting assets on blockchains.

October 2016 – Counterparty, Rare Pepes

It's just a matter of time for memes to join the blockchains. In Oct. 2016, people started to issue "rare pepes" as assets on Counterparty. The rare pepe is a kind of meme with an intense fanbase and features the frog character. There was even a meme exchange called the Rare Pepe Meme Directory.

Fig 1.1 Pepe the Frog

The Rare Pepe Meme Directory has shown the rareness of these Pepe memes and people's desire for unique digital items

March 2017 – Ehereum, Rare Pepes

As Ethereum was gaining popularity in early 2017, memes began to be traded there too. In Mar. 2017, a project called Peperium was launched to be the "decentralized trading card game and meme marketplace allowing the public to create memes that live on Ethereum and IPFS forever." Rare is the ticker for the token associated with Peperium and pays listing fees and meme creation.

June 2017 – Cryptopunks

When rare pepes trading on Ethereum became popular, two creative technologists Matt Hall and John Watkinson, got the idea to create unique characters on the Ethereum blockchains. No two characters would be the same, and they limited the characters to 10,000 in total. The project was named "Cryptopunks," referring to the cypherpunks who experimented with Bitcoin precursors in the 1990s.

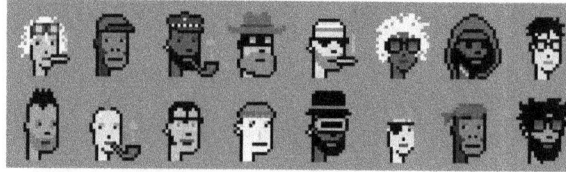

Fig 1.2 Cryptopunks

At that time, Hall and Watkinson chose to allow anyone with the Ethereum wallet to claim a Cryptopunk for free. All the 10,000 Cryptopunks were quickly claimed and led to a thriving secondary marketplace where people sold and bought them. Cryptopunks could best be considered as a hybrid of ERC20 and ERC721.

October 2017 – CryptoKitties

CryptoKitties is a kind of virtual game based on the blockchain allowing players to raise, adopt, trade virtual cats. Yes, cats on the blockchain!

This NFT soon hit the mainstream and was reported on every news station, including CoinDesk and CNN.

Fig 1.3 CryptoKitties

CrytoKitties was launched by a Vancouver-based company – Axiom Zen, in 2017. The alpha version was released during the ETH Waterloo Hackathon, the Ethereium ecosystem's largest hackathon. With over 400 developers' participation, the CryptoKitties team won first place in the hackathon; the game also went viral.

Coincidently, the 2017 crypto bull market added more fuel for the NFT fire. The public was breeding, buying, and trading virtual cats like crazy, which has opened many people's eyes to the great potential of NFTs.

Dapper Labs, another company spun out by Axiom Zen, secured 15 million dollars from top investors, including Google Ventures. After seeing top investors pour money into this company and witnessing the crazy activities in the CryptoKitties community, the public started to realize the true power of Non-Fungible Tokens.

2018-2019 - NFT Explosion

There was a massive growth of the NFT ecosystem in 2018 and 2019. More than 100 projects were created and more in the works. Non-Fungible Token marketplaces began to thrive too, such as SuperRare and OpenSea.

Although the trade volumes were relatively small compared to other crypto markets, they grew fast and have come a long way. Web3 wallets like Metamask continued to improve as well. Dapper Labs also launched a Dapper Wallet that requires no payments of gas. Other websites like ntrcryptonews.com and nonfungible.com also dive into NFT gameplay guides, market metrics and offer general information on the space.

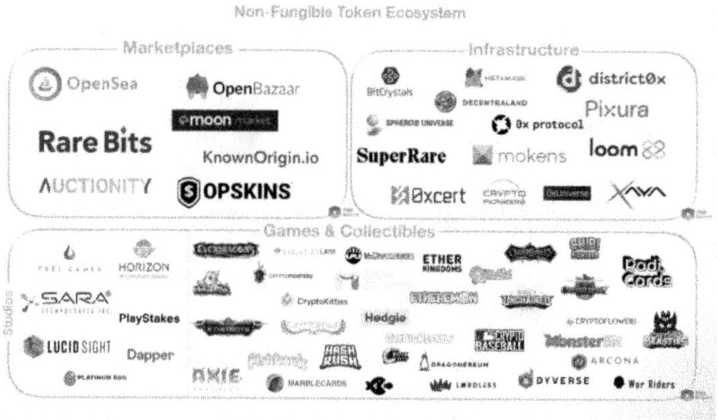

Fig 1.4 Non-Fungible Token Ecosystem

There are now endless functionalities for non-fungible tokens, including virtual clothing, character names (like domain names), even entrance tickers, virtual land plots, asteroid mining resources, and many more. The most exciting part may be the numerous NFT projects and games that collaborate to make them interoperable.

For instance, a player has an ax in one game and can be taken into another game to become a rare clothing piece. The possibilities become endless with interoperability.

1.8 Why are Non-Fungible Tokens in the Spotlight Recently?

Several factors combined:

Mainstream celebrities, including Paul Logan, are latching on the trend. The venerable auction house, Christie's sales bestow a sense of legitimacy to this. In Dec. 2020, the digital artist Beeple who was teamed with Christie made $3.5 million from his work The Complete MF Collection containing 20 art pieces.

Another major contributor: NBA Top Shot. It's a site for video-based, virtual basketball trading cards. They are sold in five-card packs and can be resold in the thriving secondary market. The owners can also display these cards they collected on publicly viewable profile sites as virtual trophy cases.

Top Shot has generated more than $200 million in sales. One of the newest records was set by 31-year-old Jesse Schwarz from Los Angeles. He bought a Lebron Moment card for $208,000 and believed he could flip the Moment for more than $1 million.

1.9 How Big is the NFT market Now?

Based on the NFT report 2020 published by Nonfungible.com and L'Atelier BNP Paribas, the NFT market value has grown by 299 percent in 2020 and is valued at over $250 million. But we already can see astonishing sales during the first months of 2021.

Chapter 2

NFT Value and Wallet

2.1 Understanding the Value of NFT and How to Increase Potential Value

Investors can use the following framework to evaluate whether the NFT is worth investing. NFT developers can apply it to increase NFTs' values to attract investors and users.

Value of and NFT = Utility + Liquidity Premium + Ownership History + Future Value

Different NFT represents different assets, and the above four NFT value components will be weighted differently too. NFTs create lots of new ways for values to be created for both asset owners and developers.

- **Utility**

How the NFT can be used decides its utility value. Two main categories that are with high utility value are tickets and game assets.

For instance, in 2019, the powerful and rare Crypto Space Commander battleship was sold for $45,250, and the NFT ticket's value is the price of the event ticket.

The other dimension of NFT utility is the **ability to use the NFT in different applications**. You can imagine that the NFT value would to definitely even higher if you can use the same battleship in different games.

However, it can be tough to realize interoperability. At present, 90% of NFT game players only play one game. This is because game developers need to build a massive game ecosystem first and then provide attractive application cases. Although many unknowns exist and may require a significant amount of time and effort, this is still exciting for the whole industry. Engin and Dapper Labs both agree and are working towards this direction.

Another easier way to increase the utility value is **forming partnerships with other businesses to offer benefits to your NFTs' holders**. For example, Dapper Labs can negotiate a discount for its CryptoKitties owners or holders by co-operating with NFT event organizers. There are technologies available like AlphaWallet's tokenScript to authenticate the owners and issuers of NFTs very efficiently. So the event organizers who would like more participants will not need to do much to implement the partnerships. This is a win-win for all parties involved.

- **Liquidity Premium**

High liquidity can be translated to a higher NFT value. The liquidity premium is the major reason why on-chain tokens should have a higher value than those created off-chain. It can be traded easily without friction with any ETH holders for ERC standard NFTs on the secondary markets, which increases the number of potential buyers.

Investors also prefer to invest in NFTs' categories with high trading volume because high liquidity will lower the risk of holding the NFT. Let's think of an extreme scenario as an example. If the NFT associated platform is closed, the NFT will lose its utility value, but a high liquid NFT will still have value as long as people are willing to sell and buy.

NFT standards that are not based on Ethereum can suffer from a lack of liquidity. The value of the NFTs created on these platforms is usually discounted.

To increase NFT liquidity and engagement, developers or creators need to design token economics that can encourage users to trade. For example, a games company can make players swap assets in order to remain competitive in the game. Also, if players are idle for too long, their NFT assets will be depreciated.

- **Ownership History**

NFT's value also depends on the identity of the issuer(s) and the previous owner(s). The NFTs with high ownership history value are usually issued or created by famous companies or artists with a strong brand.

Two main ways to increase value:

- Resell NFTs that influential people previously owned.

At present, although who are the previous owners is valuable data, it's hard to find out who they are. To increase the NFT's value, sellers and marketplaces can offer an easy-to-use tracking interface. Take OpenSea as an example, and they can not only highlight addresses of investors who made the most money from trading the NFTs but list other NFTs they own.

- Co-operate with individuals or companies with a solid brand to issue

NFT tokens

This can naturally bring users and traffic to the ecosystem. The first authorized NFT representing a Formula 1 car has been sold for $113,124.

- **Future Value**

The valuation changes and the future cash flow are the two derivations of the future value of NFTs. Valuation is often driven by speculation and sometimes is the primary driver behind price appreciation. For instance, in Dec 2017, the CryptoKitty #18's price jumped from 9 ETH to 253 ETH within only three days. Some people may argue valuation-driven price movement is negative to NFTs. However, speculation is a non-trivial part of the current financial system. Also, it's human nature to speculate. When the right balance is made, creators and developers can attract new users and increase NFT value.

Speculation and scarcity of supply drive the valuation. We can guide the speculation by highlighting NFTs that are value-appreciated and including NFT price performance charts. Let's look at the sneaker marketplace. StockX encouraged the public to speculate on the sneakers' price to create a rare sneaker market and help achieve its $1 billion valuations.

The future cash flow is the royalties or interest earned by NFT's original owner. For example, SuperRare allows NFT creators to receive 3% royalty each time their NFT artworks are sold subsequently on secondary markets.

Companies will be able to borrow concepts from innovations of DeFi in the future. To create additional cash flow, NFTs can be collateralized and leased. For example, a game player can borrow the specific game asset for one day to complete a mission.

Table 2.1 The NFT value framework's Applications

	Utility	Liquidity	Ownership History	Future Value
CryptoKitties	High	Medium	Low	Low-Medium
Euro 2020 NFT ticket	High	Medium	Low	Low

SuperRare artwork	Low	High	Medium	High
Formula 1 Delta Time car	Low	Low	High	Medium
Decentraland Property	High	High	Low	Medium-High
My Crypto Heroes hero	Low	High	Low	Medium

According to the framework, the last two Decentraland and My Crypto Heroes have the highest value, which is also confirmed by on-chain data from NonFungile.com.

Active market value = average active users * average price per asset.

In 2019, the active market value for Dectraland was 350,000 ETH and 331,260 ETH for My Crypto Heroes. The CryptoKitties' active market value was about 2,500 ETH.

2.2 Understanding Why Some NFTs are Selling for Millions of Dollars

Table 2.2 Top 10 NFT Collectible Sales in Feb. – Mar. 2021

Rank	Product	Sales	% change	Category
1	NBA Top Shot	$251,725,854	432%	Sports
2	CryptoPunks	$86,097,913	908%	Art
3	Hashmasks	$25,118,876	100%	Art
4	Sorare	$11,588,197	400%	Sports
5	Art Blocks	$7,843,263	940%	Art
6	CryptoKitties	$2,636,749	1846%	Colletible
7	Axie Infinity	$2,131,704	154%	Gaming
8	Street Fighter	$1,416,492	0%	Gaming
9	F1 Delta Time	$705,270	210%	Gaming
10	Bitcoin Origins	$334,942	43%	Collectible

DATA: Cryptoslam.io

Let's check the number one – NBA Top Shot from Dapper labs to understand why people are making millions of dollars from NFTs.

NBA Top Shot was launched in Oct. 2020 with the basketball league's backing. Users can buy digital packs containing NFTs named "moments" that are NBA highlights' short video clips, such as the memorable steal or dunk. Like physical trading cards, some moments are relatively common with more than 1,000 copies, and some can be extremely rare: only one copy.

According to the Dapper Lab's head of partnerships and marketing, Caty Tedman, the platform now already achieved more than $301m sales and 511k registered users within only five months after launching.

The rapid increase of NFTs like Top Shot is a perfect storm of several bigger trends:

1. The cryptocurrency boom and a more extensive acceptance of decentralization generated rising interests in other digital assets.
2. Covid-19 made us more plugged into virtual spaces. As more people are working from home, they are spending more time interacting in virtual spaces, which lets them become more open to the value of virtual services and goods.
3. Major institutions, including Christie's auction house, have lent NFTs prestige and credibility by joining this ecosystem.
4. The times of economic turmoil are the best periods for non-fungible goods to thrive. For example, the rare coins, we saw price spikes during the Great Depression, the 1987 stock market collapse, and the 2008 recession.

You may wonder does these NFTs really worth millions of dollars?

Like other things in the world, the value of an NFT is from extrinsic rather than intrinsic factors. For example, the intrinsic value of the CryptoPunk #6965 is almost $0, but its extrinsic value is around $1,545,929.

The major extrinsic factors we are talking about include:

1. **Utility**

Some NFTs can generate revenue, be exchanged for physical assets and other functional purposes

2. **Authencity**

For physical collectibles, most of the authentication mechanisms are efficient, which made forgeries are easily produced. However, thanks to blockchain technology, the NFT's originality is well cemented.

3. **Transferability**

NFTs can be resold to almost everyone globally, which is translated to a broader pool of potential buyers.

4. Scarcity

Quite a few NFTs are limited or one-of-a-kind. For example, there are only 10k CryptoPunks released, and only 24 are "apes." Besides, among the apes, only one dons a fedora.

5. Immutability

The metadata and code of the NFTs cannot be modified, lending it permanent.

Lots of NFT collectors are seeing the future for the tokens in rising "real world" integration. For example, with Top Shot, we may see NBA players provide meet-and-greets or court-side seats in exchange for certain moments.

2.3 Choosing Wallets to Get Started Investing NFTs
2.3.1 What is DeFi?

Simply put, Decentralized Finance (DeFi) is an ecosystem of various financial applications built on blockchain networks. Among these, the Ethereum blockchain has been the most popular one for its smart contract capabilities.

Defi's primary purpose is to create a transparent and open-source financial service ecosystem. It operates without any kind of central authority and is available to everyone. So far, the DeFi services and products include decentralized marketplaces, banking services, custodial services, decentralized exchanges, investment services, borrowing and lending, etc.

2.3.2 What is DeFi Wallet?

Defi wallet's primary purpose is to allow users to store their funds without reliance on a third party holding their assets. You have the complete freedom to do with your own funds as you please, and you are the only person in charge of your assets, which is a very revolutionary concept as you think that banks usually control your money.

With the decentralized wallet, users don't need to provide any background information to verify their identity as with centralized ones. This anonymity feature is appealing to many users since it means that your identity is never at risk. You may doubt if this is safe. In fact, DeFi wallets are the safest options available on the market. The only catch is that if you lose important login information, there will usually be no way to recover it since you are the only one in charge of your wallet.

So far, most of DeFi wallets are Ethereum-native, and the majority of DeFi tokens are supportive because they are built on the Ethereum blockchain. Web3 wallets are now the most common ones.

The core components of DeFi wallets:

1. **Key-based**

Wallets have a unique key pair. The users are responsible for keeping their private keys safe. The private keys are usually in the form of a 12 to 24-word seed phrase.

2. **Non-custodial**

Users can transfer and send assets with the understanding that they are the only ones with access to these funds

3. **Accessibility**

These wallets can hold extensive types of virtual assets. The Ehtereum-specific wallets not only allow users to deposit ETH but other DeFi tokens and stable coins.

4. **Compatibility**

Virtually all DeFi wallets are accessible by connecting to a web3 wallets. You are able to connect to DeFi applications without leaving the app.

2.3.3 How to Pick Your Defi Wallet

There are few things you can consider when choosing your Defi wallet.

1. Look at which assets the platform supports.

Different wallets support different assets, so it's critical for you to check if the wallet is compatible with whatever you want to store. If you're going to invest in NFT, do choose the ones that allow Ethereum.

2. Check the social presence of the DeFi wallets

Any reputable ones will be active on social media and are engaging with their community. So by checking out engagement and how active they are on their social medial accounts is desired.

3. Check if they allow you to lend your money and borrow capitals

With the lending feature, you can start collecting interest with the convenience of your DeFi wallet.

Besides, you should be capable of using your current funds as leverage to borrow money like USDC, DAI, or other types of money.

2.3.4 Top Defi Wallets To Get Started Investing NFTs

1. Coinbase Wallet

Coinbase is one of the best cryptocurrencies' exchanges, and the Coinbase Wallet is their DeFi application. It's very user-friendly, especially for first-time users. It's easy to buy and store tokens, transfer funds, and interact with other decentralized apps.

You will also be able to connect your <u>Coinbase wallet</u> to your <u>Coinbase account</u> and transfer the money to your wallet.

Although it's non-custodial, your private keys are kept directly on your own device, which makes it easy to recover your wallet if needed.

2. Metamask Wallet

Metamask wallet is majorly used as a browser extension that acts as the gateway to access Ethereum dApps through the internet browser. It's one of the most widely supported ones in this ecosystem.

It supports all the ERC20 tokens. Your wallet can be protected by using a hardware wallet, including Ledger as the login of Metamask.

Besides, Metamask now also has the mobile version on Android and iOs, which means you will be capable of managing your virtual assets from anywhere.

Because Metamaks is built on Ethereum blockchain and has over one million registered users, it is one of the best non-custodial wallets out there.

Metamask is most popular for easy and small transactions. It might be for those who store the significant value of DeFi funds.

3. Trust Wallet

Trust wallet has a variety of interconnected DeFi items. You can use BinanceDex's advanced exchange function or swap assets in your App with BinanceDex or KeyberSwap.

The Android version of Trust wallet has built-in Dapp browsers allowing you full access to the Defi environment. You are able to visit DeFi websites and connect with your wallet balance without exiting the App.

WaterConnect is used as an open protocol to link Dapps to mobile wallets by checking the QR code. Use WaterConnect, and you can connect your Trust wallet to Dapps and make safe transactions without the need to share any confidential information.

4. Enjin Wallet

Enjin wallet is compatible with crypto assets, especially the in-game ones. It encompasses some of the most innovative security methods by using unique characteristics, including intuitive UI, address management, and login with the fingerprints. It's available for both Apple and Android systems.

This wallet allows you to store ERC1155 and ERC721 blockchain-based game collectibles.

While It's not open-source, so the code is not visible and editable for its users. There's no multi-signature feature, which means transactions won't need more people to sign them.

Chapter 3

Investing By Creating NFTs

3.1 Should You Create Your Own NFT Artworks?

You probably doubt whether or not NFTs are worth a shot. When you think of the traditional art world, you see various art galleries, people spending hundreds of thousands or even millions on artworks. But then you get struck by the reality. There are only a countable few people who can make a living out of this. Even then, their revenues have to be shared with other parties involved in the sale.

However, the NFT world can be different. As the artists, you will be able to control all strings of your artwork. Since NFTs' marketplaces are global, your artwork will be exposed to the whole world. There's no need to contact an agency or a gallery to sell your work. You also don't have to share your revenue with multiple parties or middlemen. The NFTs' marketplaces will keep you in your artwork's sale loop all the time. You will be able to get a fair commission from every NFT artwork you sell. Besides, at any time, you are capable of proving the authenticity of your art, and there's only one person to be the true owner of your artwork at a given time. In fact, the entire NFT artwork ecosystem provides a more democratic landscape for everybody to create, buy and sell artwork.

Also, unlike in the traditional art world, where you get paid in weeks or months after selling the artworks, you will receive the money instantly into your crypto wallet as soon as you make the NFT artwork sale. This is real excitement and relief.

What makes it even better? If your initial collector gets an offer on the art and decides to sell it. Boom! Another 10% (for example) of the resale value will immediately appear in your crypto wallet in most services.

NFT makes it more convenient for those motion-based and 3D artworks. These kinds of art are hard to sell as physical pieces and shown best in digital form.

Your artworks will also be viewed from anywhere, and you can avoid issues of shipping.

So, what are the downsides?

Your artwork will be tossed into a vast sea of art. Like other online businesses, you will still need to bring your work to the attention of potential buyers and collectors.

If you lose your crypto wallet login information, unlike the traditional banks that can help you reset your password, you will lose your artworks and money forever.

Another "gas fee" is associated with each transaction of Etherium that can quickly be added up. Although some companies are working hard on keeping down the price of the electricity used to create and track every crypto art piece, the cost is not ideal.

On balance, it is still worth you dipping your toes in the crypto art pond. Tokenizing your artwork doesn't mean you lose your intellectual rights. You will always be able to sell your artworks traditionally- print them, show and sell them physically. The most you will lose is the gas fee and some time.

3.2 Can Your Content Be an NFT?

Probably.

Almost anything goes in the NFT, like memes, songs, recipes, digital art, and even entire startups are listed on the NFT marketplaces now. There are currently very few restrictions regarding what types of content can be tokenized and turned into NFTs.

As digital art's demand continues to grow, it's a great time to experiment with this technology for your artwork. One rule that should be kept in mind is that avoiding turning copyrighted assets or contents into NFTs.

3.3 What Needed to Start Creating NFTs? Step-by-Step Instructions

You won't need extensive crypto knowledge to create NFTs, while you do need several tools to get started. It's Okay if you are not familiar with them yet. You will be able to get everything set up in only a few minutes from your phone. Let's get started.

In this section, you will learn to set up a crypto wallet, purchase ETH, and connect your crypto wallets to NFT marketplaces.

Step 1: Set Up Your Ethereum Wallet

What's your first step in your NFT journey? It's to create a digital wallet where you can securely store your cryptocurrency used to create, buy, and sell NFTs. This crypto wallet will also allow you to create accounts and safely sign-in on NFT marketplaces.

Hundreds of platforms provide free wallets that can help you store cryptocurrencies. In Chapter 2, the section of 2.3 Choosing Wallets to Get Started Investing NFTs, we have introduced how to choose and the top ones that work well with most major blockchain apps and NFT marketplaces.

Step 2: Buy A Small Amount of Ehtereum (ETH)

There will be fees associated with turning your artwork into NFTs on most major digital art marketplaces. So you will need to buy some ETH to cover the costs of making your first NFT.

Since the ETH's price fluctuates almost every second, it's challenging to track it. One easier way to get started is by choosing your funds in dollar with the amount you are willing to purchase and invest exactly that much ETH. The Metamask introduced before allows you to buy crypto right inside your crypto wallet. In contrast, the <u>Coinbase wallet</u> needs you to purchase from another exchange platform and transfer it into your wallet.

Step 3: Connect The Crypto Wallet To NFT Marketplaces

After you set up your wallet and buy some ETH, it's time to choose a marketplace where you want to make NFTs and list your work. For beginners who just started, <u>Rarible</u> is an excellent choice as they have the most straightforward and most effortless setup.

To connect your crypto wallet to __Rarible__, go to their site and click the **Connect** button in the screen's top right corner.

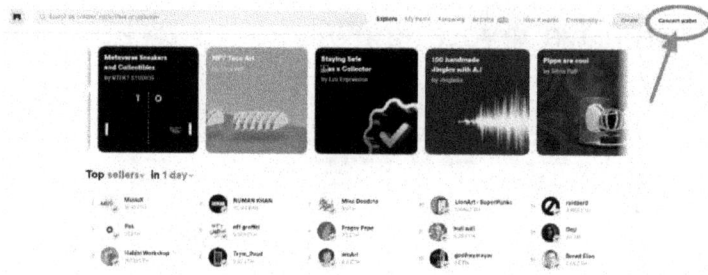

Fig 3.1 Connect crypto wallet to Rarible

On the next screen, choose the wallet you decided on in the previous step.

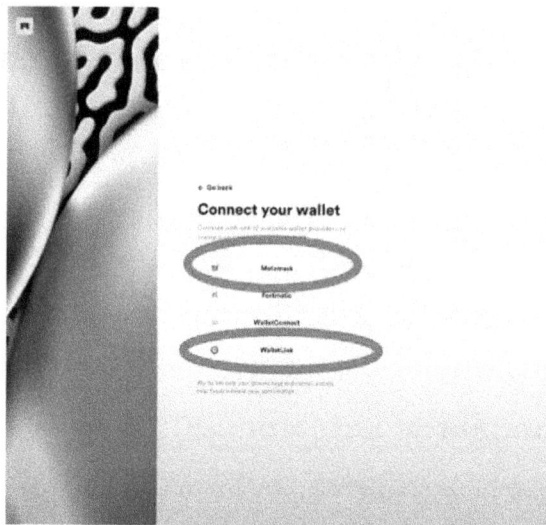

Fig 3.2 Choose your wallet

No matter which wallet you chose, the next step is almost the same. A QR code will appear on the screen after you select your connection wallet. Then use your crypto wallet app to scan this code. After you scan the code, confirm that you would like to connect your crypto wallet to Rarible.

This is a safe connection, and Rarible will always make you confirm purchases with your crypto wallet apps before moving forward with anything. Your Rarible account will be instantly generated once you connect to the wallet.

Now you have everything needed to create and sell your first NFT.

3.4 How to Create NFT Art With No Coding Experience
Step 1: Make a Digital Art File as NFTs

No standard technique is there to create a piece of art that can be used as NFTs. As long as the file you created is supported by the marketplace you are using to list it, it will work as NFTs.

This contains lots of opportunities for the content you can monetize. On Rarible or Zora, the image as JPG, PNG, TXT, or GIF, MP3 can be NFTs. A meme can be an NFT too. Construct a tasty recipe and have it saved as the TXT? There's an NFT.

Here, we are going to use __Rarible__, with no coding experience needed.

First, Click the "Create Collectibles" in the upper right corner.

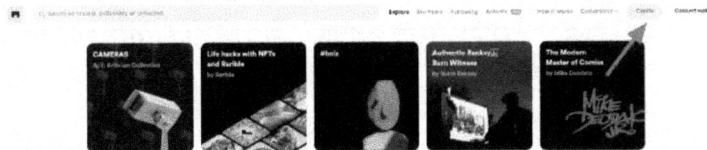

Fig 3.3 Click "Create Collectibles" on Rarible

Then we're going to see we can either create a single collectible or multiple. So we can have one rare, or we can make multiple collectibles. So let's do multiple.

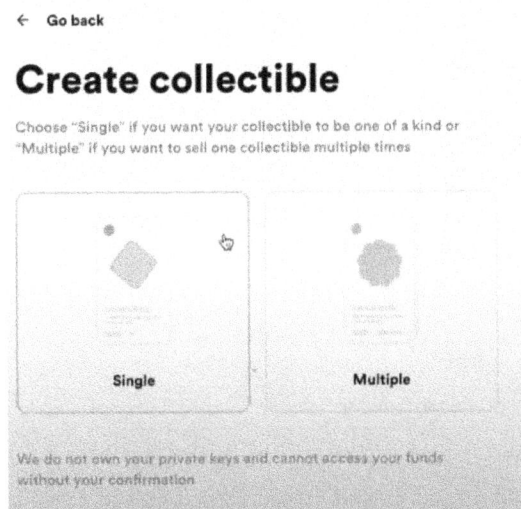

Fig 3.4 Create Collectible

We're going to do multiple and start from scratch, and it's going to say select an image: jpg, png, or a gif. So you can use any file as long as it is a jpeg, png, or gif. It could be a picture you took on your phone, and it can also be a picture you took several years ago that you uploaded onto your computer with a scanner any file that meets these criteria.

If you have a file already or a picture that you want to turn into an NFT, you can upload it right here but let's say you have a file or an image that is not part of these formats. It's straightforward to convert them. You can go to onlineconvert.com, and you can convert an image to a png file or a jpeg file.

After you get the file in the acceptable format, you can go and upload it to Rarible.

Please note that they recommend that the file should be under 10 megabytes, so if you do have a file that is above 10 megabytes and want to compress it, go to tinypng.com. You can take a png file or a jpeg file, and you can compress it here. Once we have those images, we can go back to Rarible, and we can upload them.

But let's say you want to create an image from scratch. I prefer using Canva. It is where I do my own work. Canva is a great software. There is a free version, and also there is the paid version which is about ten dollars per month.

Another helpful tool is Kapwing. It provides several tools well suited to help you create and get more from your existing NFTs.

Here, let's make a quick piece of NFT with Canva to upload to Rarible.

So we're going to create a design. We'll do a logo here, but you can do any art, or you could do Instagram posts, Facebook posts, brochures, anything you can think of.

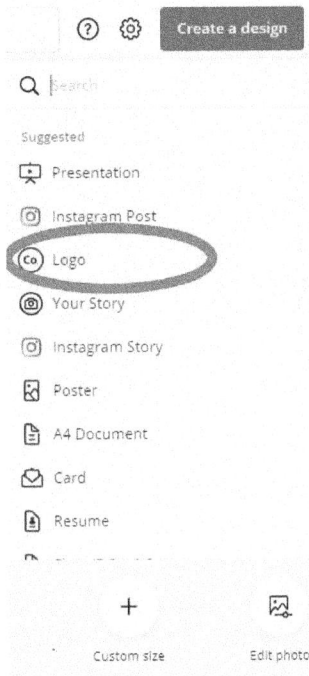

Fig 3.5 Create Design

Let's make a crypto monkey. First, choose the monkey you like, and we can enlarge it. You can do whatever you want on <u>Canva</u>. It's very easy to use.

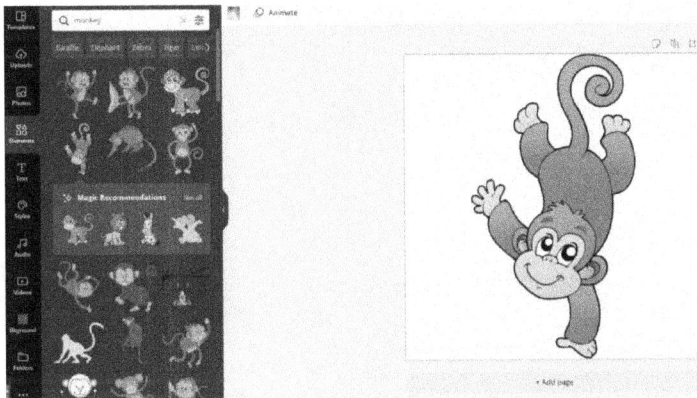

Fig 3.6 Create a monkey

We'll get an Ethereum logo. Now, this is our NFT.

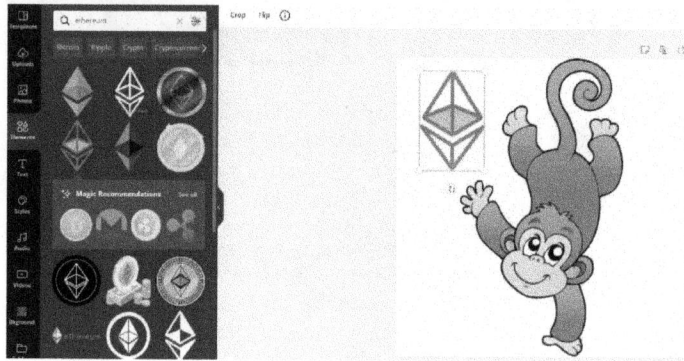
Fig 3.7 Add ETH logo

Next, let's save it and download it. We'll call it crypto monkey.

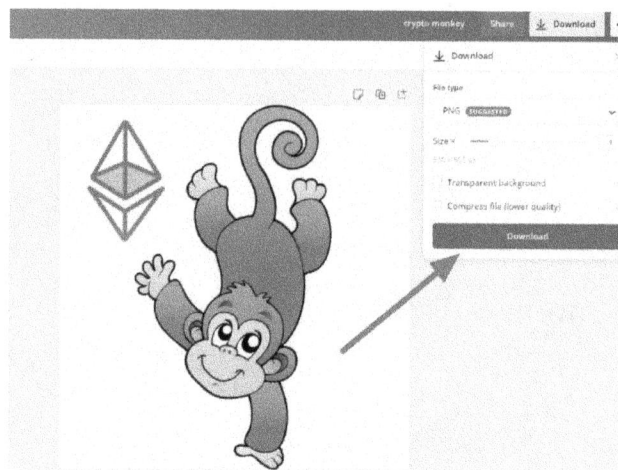
Fig 3.8 Save & download your work

Step 2: Upload the artwork to Rarible.

We now have our png file. So let's go back to Rarible, and let's upload it. We're going to choose our image of the crypto monkey.

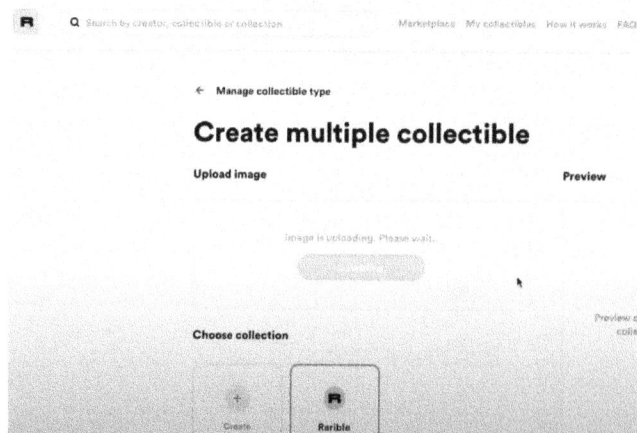
Fig 3.9 Create NFT on Rarible

We can also choose a collection on this page, or you can keep it on Rarible.

We can also give it a **name**, so we're going to call it crypto monkey Super. Then we can do an optional **description**: this is a crypto monkey Super, or whatever you want. Then over here, we can choose how many copies we want. Since we did multiple collectibles, so we can do multiple copies here.

Another thing we can set up here is **royalties**. This means that after you sell your NFT to someone, you will receive a royalty every time it is sold. They recommend or suggested 10, 20, or 30 percent.

For **properties,** this will depend on what you're actually creating. For example, we'll do our property as the animal for our crypto monkey. You can go as heavy on this as you want, and you can create properties, or you can create no properties; that's up to you.

Then we're going to set a price for it. Please note there's a service fee of 2.5 percent.

For **unlock once purchase,** don't touch that; just leave that as it is.

After you check your **preview** to make everything looks correct and then click **Create**.

Attention: this is where we run into the risk or the issue of creating NFTs.

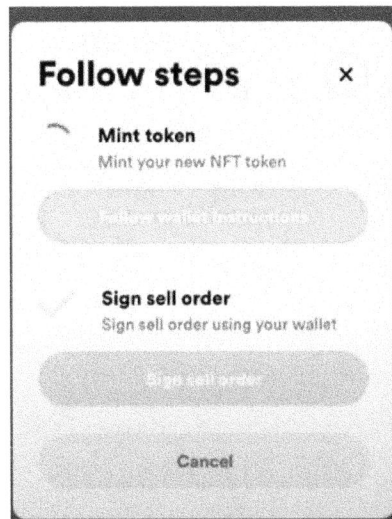

Fig 3.10 Mint & Sell NFT on Rarible

You might have come to this, and you want to sell it at a high price. You may want to create a hundred of these NFTS, maybe a thousand, and think of one of them will eventually sell. However, the problem is every time you create an NFT, there is a transaction on the ETH blockchain, so you're going to pay a **gas fee**. Right now, the gas fee to mint this token is six dollars and twenty-one cents, which you might consider very low, but I've seen these gas fees for nine dollars ten dollars and even more.

AMOUNT + GAS FEE

TOTAL   ◆0.016329

$6.21

Fig 3.11 Gas fee example

Actually, six dollars is still a lot of money to create an NFT that likely won't sell. It's important to understand the NFT art market before creating these because You might end up creating a hundred of these tokens, and the cost was seven dollars here, ten dollars there, and they add up to hundreds of dollars.

Okay, after we **confirm** this and our first NFT is successfully created!

Step 3: Wait for Bids.

Once you list the art, anyone can find it and place the bid for your NFTs. Most platforms also require creators to check back for bids and won't notify you when one comes in. This is a growing issue that hopefully will get solved in the near future.

Discoverability can vary a lot across these major marketplaces, and if you want your work to get more exposure, you need to promote your work by yourself. Most NFT marketplaces like Rarible, SuperRare have a large associated community or Discord built around them to help your promoting.

3.5 Why It Can Be Expensive To Create NFTs?

It requires an innovative one-of-a-kind digital currency to be minted on the blockchain to turn a piece of content into the NFT. This creation process requires a fairly complicated computational task with an entire computer network.

To create your NFTs using the ETH network, you need to pay the "gas fee" mentioned above for the effort and energy that goes into the computation. The gas fee price also fluctuates every day, and it can be at a higher price compared to your work's sale price.

In fact, these frequently ludicrous fees are problematic if we think of the broader adoption of NFT technology. It would be best if these issues can be ironed out and in the future. As more and more NFT artists continue to emerge in this field, marketplaces are also exploring more alternative ways to reduce the gas fees for the creators and artists.

3.6 How To Create NFTs for Free without Gas Fees

Now you may feel that the gas fees are a pain for artists and creators. Also, the gas fees are the number one complaint from creators and users. Fortunately, some platforms have released gasless minting. Here, we are going to introduce two popular ones.

Mintable

Currently, as you create a new NFT on Mintable, you will be given an extra choice to make the transaction-free NFT or the traditional one.

Signing a message is all you will need to do to create your NFTs. So beginners who are not willing to spend money upfront will be able to start trying the NFT space. Compared to the traditional way, now you can do it completely free of the gas fees.

According to Mintable, you can do everything you usually do with the NFTs, including:

- Batch Minting
- Making all kinds of NFTs, from music, video, to access tokens, etc.
- Uploading private files with 300mb file limitation, and images with 100mb limit. Files can be uploaded as jpg, MP3, MP4, GLB, and zip files.

If the buyer purchases your NFT, they will need to pay for the listed purchase price and the gas fee for the buying transaction.

Another noticeable difference regarding the tracking is that the NFT will not show up in your wallet until transferred or purchased. This is because the way the crypto wallets view for NFTs is by listening for a transfer event. If there are no transactions shown on the blockchain, there's no record. The transfer event only happens when you transfer it to someone else or yourself, or someone purchases it. You don't need to worry. The work still exists. It's still shown on Mintable and Etherscan. Depending on the wallet you're using, if you manually add it to your wallet, you can see it.

Starting creating NFTs on Mintable for Free:

1. Go to the Mintable.app
2. In the right upper section, you will find the **sell** button and click it.
3. Choose to create a new item, then choose **gasless**.

Traditional or gasless?

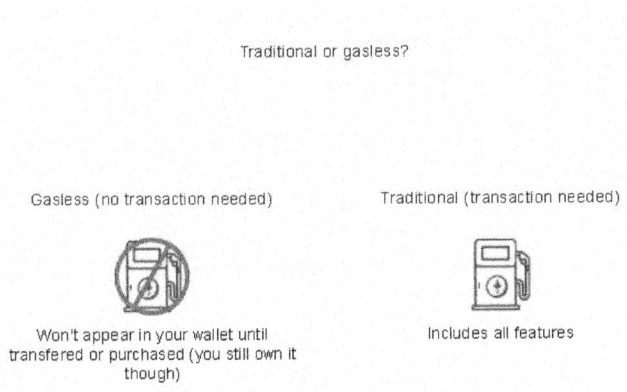

Gasless (no transaction needed)

Won't appear in your wallet until transfered or purchased (you still own it though)

Traditional (transaction needed)

Includes all features

Fig 3.12 Traditional or Gasless

4. Connect your crypto wallet and login, then create your first NFT!

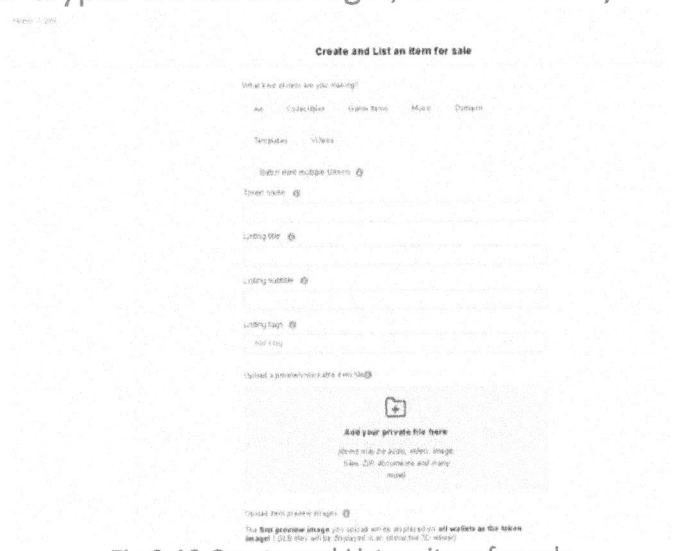

Fig 3.13 Create and List an item for sale

OpenSea

Another popular one is OpenSea. They have announced **Collection Manager**, which allows you to make your NFTs entirely for free, with no gas fees needed. Selling NFTs are also gasless. What you need to do is just initializing your OpenSea Account once.

The Collection Manager not only allows creators to mint NFTs without any upfront gas fees but creates collections for free and instantly.

Starting creating NFTs with Collections on OpenSea for Free:

After you set up your account and connect with your crypto wallet:

1. Go to <u>https://opensea.io/collections</u>, create a collection and choose it.

2. The **Edit** button and an **Add New Item** button will appear

For the **Edit** button, it allows you to:

* Choose which currencies, including social tokens that you prefer to use on your store

* Configure your social media links, logos, and display settings

* Configure the commissions that you want to take on first and secondary sales

For Add New Item button, it is to create a new NFT:

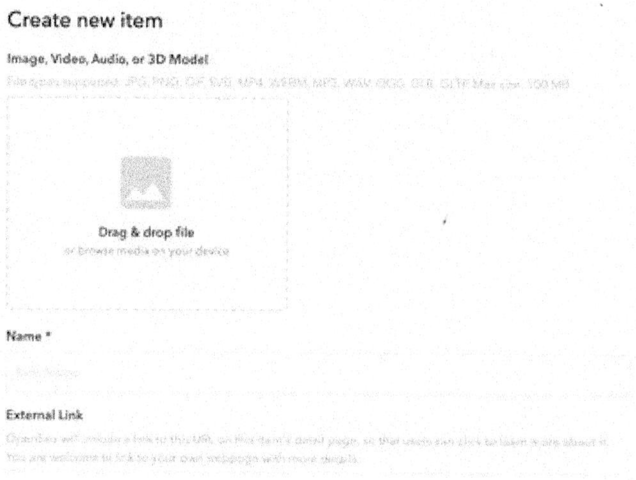

Fig 3.14 Crete new NFT on OpenSea

The NFTs you make with the Collection Manager of OpenSea follow the <u>ERC-1155</u> standard. Once you create the NFT, you encode its total supply and your address in the token's ID, which means no one except you will be able to make more of them. The buyers will be counted on a hard cap on supply which is enforced by code.

If you want to manage the way your NFTs look on OpenSea or deploy your own contracts, or set sale commissions and currencies you prefer, you can do those through the same interface.

Another question now may pop up:

Won't this gasless feature increase the spam or amount of low-quality NFTs?

These platforms have foreseen this issue and are taking action. For example, Mintable is releasing a new voting system to better view and browse high-quality NFTs, which can help superb quality NFTs get more exposure or views and find more potential buyers.

3.7 Related Legal Issues Worth Your Attention

As we have noticed, anyone can make NFTs of anything worldwide, even if the contents don't belong to them. However, this brings the questions of copyright infringement and copyfraud to us.

Copyright Infringement

You may think creating NFTs from the public domain works is interesting, while the issue that probably generates legal conflicts is creating the work from a person that is not its owner or the author. Another problematic phenomenon appearing is that people began to create pieces that do not belong to them.

The artist, CorbinRanbolt, has complained that some of his dinosaurs' artworks have been tokenized without his permission. Another artist WerdUndead had their works created and placed in OpenSea by someone else.

In both situations, the artworks have been removed from the NFT marketplaces, but it made us ask whether or not it is copyright infringement for the authorized creation of a work.

Creating and selling NFTs based on the artworks you don't own or hold the right to is an infringement. This is why the auction sites of NFT have rushed to create DMCA processes for removing those unauthorized ones. However, it's not that clear if this is enough that many sites are now actively encouraging the public to tokenized content that doesn't belong to them. Some marketplaces only allow verified work, which makes it less worrisome in this industry.

Artists are allowed to make derivative works based on their own creations and sell them. As long as buyers are fully aware the NFTs are useless practically, there's not enough reason for the courts to get involved.

However, as we see the NFT industry boom, we are now also seeing far more concerns regarding copyright infringement, and the system is getting abused.

What makes it more complicated is that even when the original artists don't care, you use their works first, but they can still sue you at the end of the day. Because the artwork owners can change their mind at any point in the future, and you are using their work in a way they're not happy about. A typical and interesting case example was that in 2019, InfoWars paid Pepe the Frog creator Matt Furie $15,000 to settle the lawsuit against them. One of the important lessons left for us is that creators should avoid making public statements saying they do not care about their copyrights or tolerance for unauthorized uses. So if you sell other people's art for millions of dollars, they will certainly have the right to come after you. Another lesson is that virality or meme-ification will not decrease the copyright's strength. Actually, the works' authorships are entitled to the same types of protections, no matter what form of use- online, print, social media, whatever it can be. For example, if you see a meme going viral on social media, everybody is using it or joking about it, but this doesn't mean you are safe to transfer to your NFT and sell it.

Copyfraud

This term refers to making a dubious or false copyright claim over works in the public domain. Yes, public domain works can be used by anyone. However, sometimes an institution will claim the copyright over such works. The Global Art Museum (GAM) has tokenized some public domain works and listed them for sales on OpenSea. Although there might not be a legal issue with copyfraud taking place, we need to ask if the GAM's tokenization of works can even be copyfraud. Now we already knew, if one person makes an NFT of a picture or image, he/she has to have the original file used to create the token. In GAM's case, they took artworks from the public domain's digital artwork collection at the Rijiksmeusm in Amsterdam. This collection is a celebrated and famous one that has gone completely digital and is marked as being in the public domain.

Also, the Rijksmuseum encourages re-uses of their works, which is a strong political statement in the public domain's defense. While one should not enclose the public domain since it's for everyone. The Rijksmuseum has claimed ownership of all the photographs of their artworks. However, it doesn't seem to be interested in enforcing it.

GAM also stated clearly that all the works are from the Rijksmuseum and don't claim any of the institution's involvement. So there're no ownership claims, only creating a unique version of the works that are not even a copy of the works themselves. This is not copyfraud.

The NFTs have a cryptographic sign to make the file unique, and this sign is not even from the author (since the artists of the public domain's works are no longer with us.) This is like you purchased something and tell others you own exclusive metadata, which others can reproduce. You may see it as pointless at best or slightly unethical at worst.

Could NFTs Help Rightsholders or Creators?

Simply put, yes. NFTs not only give creators another innovative potential revenue stream by selling their works' unique copies but help keep track of ownership of copyrights.

In theory, creators can create the works, tokenize them, and keep the token both as proof of copyright ownership and creation. They are able to transfer this token as part of the copyright transfer. In reality, however, this is not how it's usually used. It's often used just to create some "special" works' copies and sell those copies. Usually, it's not the creators who are reaping those rewards.

Currently, this is something artists and creators need to explore both as potential piracy threats and business opportunities. If your NFT works need to capture the scarcity and uniqueness that this technology can bring to you, they need to be scarce and not just something anyone is capable of conjuring up.

Chapter 4

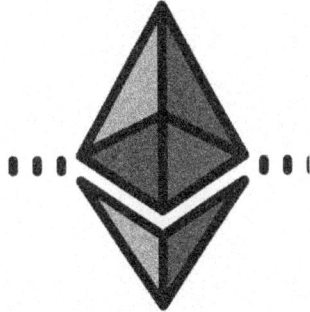

Investing by Buying NFTs

Maybe you're not an artist, or perhaps you are not interested in being NFT creators. Buying and collecting NFTs is another excellent choice for you.

4.1 What Do You Get When You Purchase NFTs?

Once you buy an NFT, you own the digital rights of its digital asset, whether image or music. This can be proven in two ways: buyers get the single token bequeathing the ownership, and every NFT is uploaded to the digital ledger to be tracked as it's made, bought, and sold.

The pride and ability for holders to say they own the original work bring much value to NFTs. The president of Nonfungible.com, Dan Kelly, said, "The real key is the ownership itself. It is the status coming with owning the NFT. It's very different owning the original versus the replica."

The main reason making people hesitant about purchasing NFTs is the assumption that having the collectible's physical version is more valuable than the digital one. While NFTs are usually more secure due to their authentication process. Ethereum is the primary platform on which most NFTs are made due to its flexibility for creators to store blockchain projects' codes.

Before purchasing NFTs, you also need to understand:

4.2 What Makes an NFT original?

The rights of the original asset only belong to the buyer of the NFT. However, other copies can still be floating online and for free. Mr.Kelly compares this to owning the original version of Mona Lisa and the floating reprints. He said only one person has the original.

NFTs' ownership rights are the details that are currently being ironed out in the United States. Now, when the individual acquires the NFT, he/she owns the underlying asset, but not the work's copyright.

According to Ali Dhanani, the intellectual property lawyer at Baker Botts, if buyers want all rights to the collectible, the copyright holder will need to transfer the copyright by contract separately. Without this transfer, the copyright creator can still separately display, use, distribute, or even create reprints of the artwork, including creating new NFTs for these reprints.

4.3 How Much Do You Need to Spend?

This varies, and a lot. Some can be bought for as little as a few dollars, and others can cost as much as millions of dollars at auction. For example, the NFTs of the Kings of Leon albums were sold for $50. While the Nyan Cat meme that describes a cat with the Pop-Tart body sold for almost $600,000. One man has spent more than $175,000 on NBA Top Shot trading cards, but now they are worth $20 million.

4.4 Where & How You Can Buy and Sell NFTs
1. Within the Application

CryptoKitties

Let's look at so far one of the most popular ones – CryptoKitties. Cryptokitties are digital kittens that you can breed, customize, buy and sell. Using the application is simple. All you need to do is go to **cryptokitties.co**, or you could google CryptoKitties, and it'll bring you to this website.

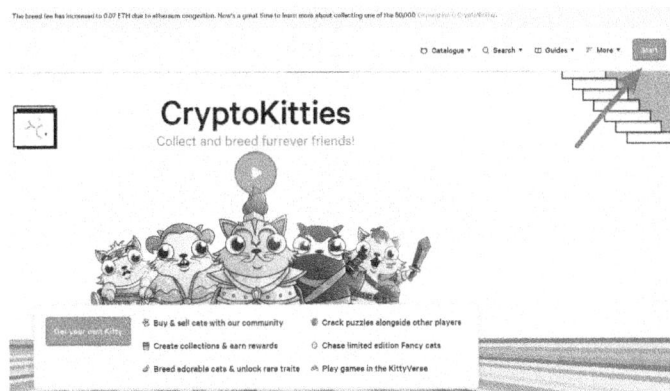

Fig 4.1 CryptoKitties Page

After you connect your MetaMask wallet, you join the CryptoKittes and can start buying, selling, and customizing them.

If you don't have a MetaMask wallet, please check the previous chapter for more details. Crypto wallets enable you to access applications such as CryptoKitties or other NFT applications. There are other wallets that interact with these protocols, but for the most part, MetaMask is the go-to since it will work most likely across all platforms.

After you finish the setup, feel free to explore these applications. You will go through several confirmations that you are actually authorizing the confirmation or transaction. If it's the first time you log in with a wallet, it will bring you through a little tutorial. Or once you're connected, you can go to **Guides** and choose the **kitten Class**.

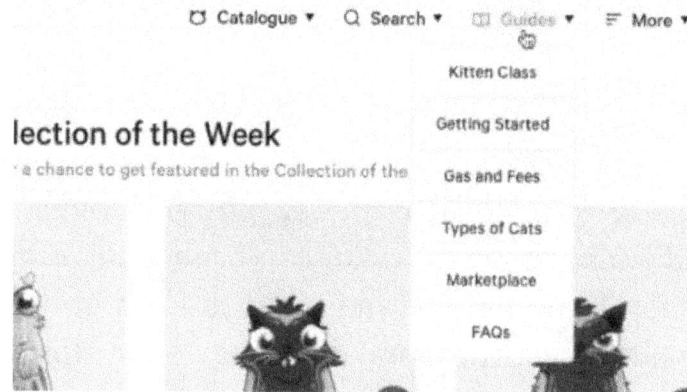

Fig 4.2 CryptoKitties Guides

After you learn how to play with this, you're free to begin. Please note that every time we make a transaction like buying a kittie, there will be a gas fee. Sometimes these fees are so high, and maybe the transaction might not be worth it. Any transaction on Ethereum will require gas. For example, if you want to buy a crypto kitty for $3.42, there's a transaction fee of $5.78.

The crypto kitty is not stored on this website nor the computer. The control to this NFT or this crypto kitty is under your MetaMask wallet. This means we can take our MetaMask wallet to a whole different platform and bring our crypto kitty along with us. The MetaMask wallet we're using is our profile is how we log in to new NFT platforms or new marketplaces. You can list your crypto kitties on other marketplaces like OpenSea to sell them.

Now, let's look at another within-application example:

Decentraland

Decentraland is a virtual world where you can buy virtual land and virtual items such as hats, pens, sweatshirts, etc.

Entering the Decentraland is the same way as we enter into other applications such as CryptoKitties. We go to the website decentraland.org, we click "Get Started," and we're going to connect our MetaMask wallet the same way as we did it before.

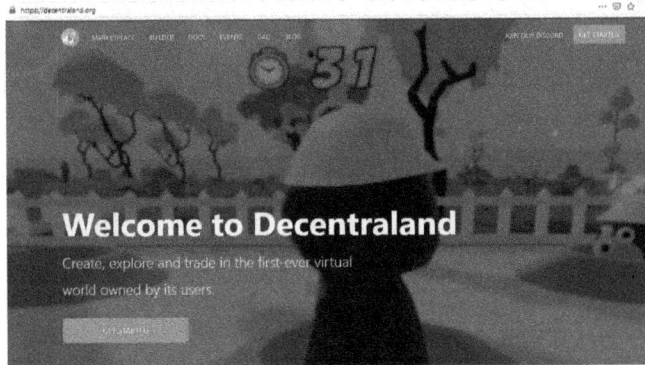
Fig 4.3 Decentraland

After you confirm your legal age and agree to the terms of services and privacy policy, you start exploring.

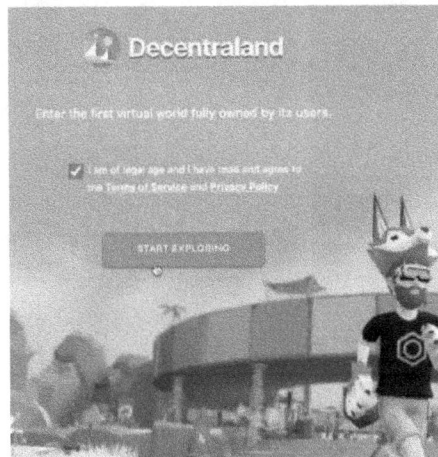
Fig 4.4 Decentraland Start Exploring

It is important to know that there are many images and graphics, so it does take a while to load, and eventually, you will enter into that world.

In the Decentraland marketplace, when you check the prices, they might look very high to you, but they're not.

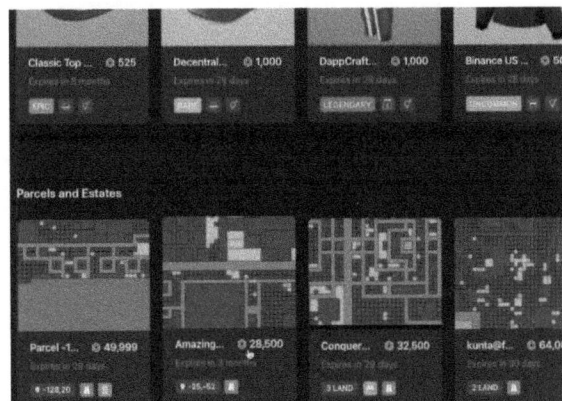

Fig 4.5 Decentraland marketplace example

These are priced in the token **MANA**, the digital asset token used for services and goods in Decentraland. The MANA to USD rate for today is 0.960330. You can buy MANA on <u>Gemini</u>, and then transfer it over to your MetaMask wallet. You can buy MANA on <u>BINANCE.US</u>. If you don't have MANA, and you still want to buy these assets for Decentraland. You can still do that through OpenSea.

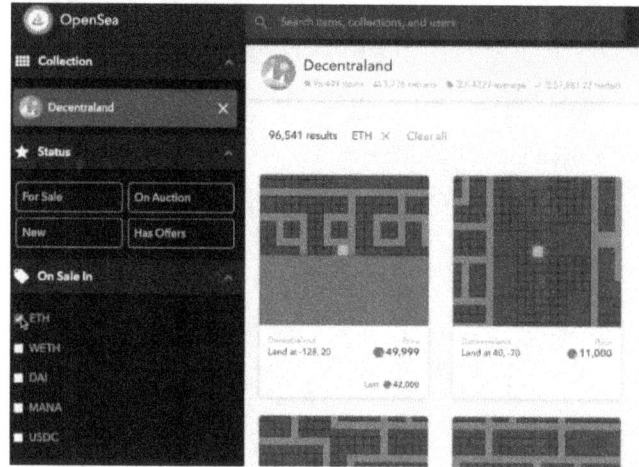

Fig 4.6 Decentraland on OpenSea

On OpenSea, you can buy decentralized essential land NFTs, and on the left-hand side, you can narrow it down to payments in Ethereum.

On Decentraland, it's almost like a real-world, but it's virtual. We can make houses, buy lands and things of that nature. You can also choose to jump into another new word from the button on the right-hand corner.

Best For Sports Fans: NBA Top Shot

The NBA Top Shot is the digital answer to sports' collectibles and the future for memorabilia of sports. It has hot again for the past few years.

Fig 4.7 NAB Top Shot

NAB Top shot allows users to own the most memorable and best moments from NBA history. Sports fans can collect and bid on three categories of the top moments: Vets, Rookies, and Rising Star Players. You will also see a wide range of collection and edition' sizes.

For the top-tier genesis, only one edition of collectible is for sale. For the lowest tier, like Memorabilia, there are 10,000+ editions available.

This marketplace is easy to navigate. You can search by moments from your favorite teams or by categories like lastest drop moments. Also, you will be able to search by tier, player, or set to find the exact kind of collectible moments you look for.

2. Through open marketplaces

Online marketplaces are for buyers to make purchases, take part in auctions, and sell NFTs. NFTs can be resold on the same marketplaces. It's recommended that beginners stick to buy from primary market sites directly from vendors. It will get trickier to verify the authenticity on other secondary sites if you're not familiar with the buying and selling process.

Best For Variety: OpenSea

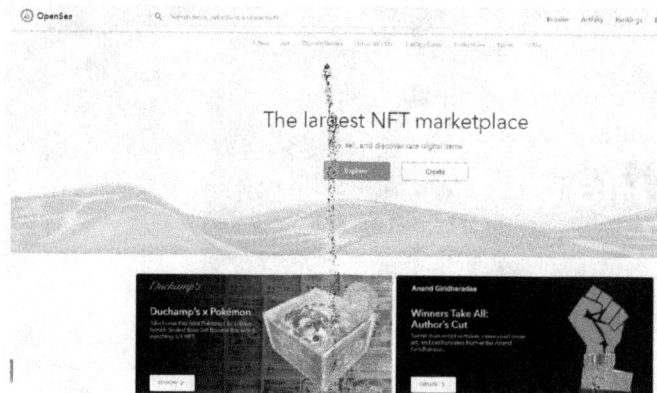
Fig 4.8 OpenSea First Page

OpenSea is one of the earliest NFT marketplaces and now is the largest one in operation. It features a massive library of content, and you can browse all kinds of NFTs, from items used in video games, digital art to rare collectibles. OpenSea is entirely open to newcomers, and it's easier to get started. It has one of the best experiences for viewing and browsing items.

Similar to other exchanges, OpenSea is built on Ethereum. To funds your bides, trades, or cover other fees that may occur, you need to buy ETH. While this is often cents on the dollar at most. You will also need an active crypto wallet, and MetaMesk is an excellent choice.

Best for Exclusive Drops: <u>Nifty Gateway</u>

Fig 4.9 Nifty Gateway First Page

Nifty Gateway is powered by Gemini and is a highly curated NFT marketplace focusing on digital collectibles. It works with high-profile musicians and artists like Justin Roiland to release limited edition NFT collections. You can also have alerts set for any of your favorite artists and brands when they drop new merch.

Nifty is also the only major NFT marketplace that accepts credit cards, which separates it from other digital marketplaces. The arts on NFT are usually expensive. New artists will also need to apply before they are capable of posting here.

Nifty is also perfect for those who obsess over exclusive drops from those iconic brands like Supreme. You can sign up for the exclusive drop list or check out its drop schedule to keep an eye on new releases from super-sought creators like Marius Sperlich and EDM musician Deadmau5.

How to See What's for Sale on Nifty?

Unfortunately, you cannot see much of what will be listed for sale until the releasing date. On its drops page, Nifty has a lineup of which artists are going to release NFTs, and you can check the date and time for each one. Typically, it's 7 p.m for on weekdays' releases, and 2 p.m for weekends' releases.

Another good way to get an idea of what's being released is by following your favorite artists on their social media platforms. The artists sometimes won't specify the detailed prices, the number of prints, or edition versions before the release day, so you need to go to Nifty to preview the drop on the release day.

Best for Social Aspect: <u>SuperRare</u>

Fig 4.10 SuperRare First Page

SuperRare is a digital artwork auction house with social networks. It values socially-driven artworks, which makes sense. Since NFTs are speculative in nature, and the artwork's fans like you and I decide their values. It's challenging to assign the value without others desire the same pieces or understanding why other collectors get crazy for the piece.

The collections on SuperRare are highly curated. The team is intentionally slow on getting new creators on board, which will make buyers feel like stepping into an elite digital gallery. The NFTs shown on this platform are stunning and reflect thousands of hours of artists' effort. New creators are only accepted with the **application**, and the prices of the NFTs can get very steep.

Most Accessible for New Collectors: Rarible

Rarible is the most accessible to new creators and collectors, which leads to a grab bag of artworks on its site. It hosted more than 30,000 users at the beginning of 2021. Sales for artwork vary widely with NFTs from a few dollars to tens of thousands.

Other marketplaces that you can buy NFTs include:

- Foundation
- BakerySwap
- Axie Marketplace
- Zora
- VIV3
- NFT ShowRoom

4.5 How To Find Valuable NFTs

Some NFTs were selling for hundreds of thousands of dollars, and you might be wondering how I can get my hands on one of these valuable NFTs. This can be tricky, and the following are three methods on how you can find valuable NFTs.

1. Studying the Popular Platforms

If we look at some of the most expensive NFTs sold, we can see they happen to sell within the same platforms. When you check the most expensive game NFTs as shown below, you can notice that Axie Infinity, F1 Delta Time, and Sorare repeatedly appear on the rank list.

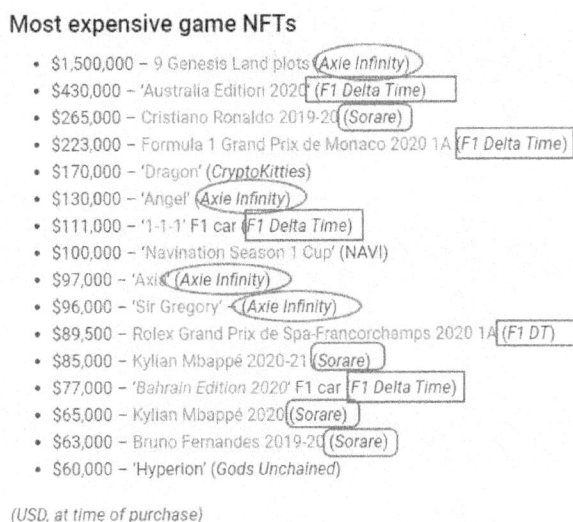

Most expensive game NFTs

- $1,500,000 – 9 Genesis Land plots (*Axie Infinity*)
- $430,000 – 'Australia Edition 2020' (*F1 Delta Time*)
- $265,000 – Cristiano Ronaldo 2019-20 (*Sorare*)
- $223,000 – Formula 1 Grand Prix de Monaco 2020 1A (*F1 Delta Time*)
- $170,000 – 'Dragon' (*CryptoKitties*)
- $130,000 – 'Angel' (*Axie Infinity*)
- $111,000 – '1-1-1' F1 car (*F1 Delta Time*)
- $100,000 – 'Navination Season 1 Cup' (*NAVI*)
- $97,000 – 'Axie' (*Axie Infinity*)
- $96,000 – 'Sir Gregory' (*Axie Infinity*)
- $89,500 – Rolex Grand Prix de Spa-Francorchamps 2020 1A (*F1 DT*)
- $85,000 – Kylian Mbappé 2020-21 (*Sorare*)
- $77,000 – 'Bahrain Edition 2020' F1 car (*F1 Delta Time*)
- $65,000 – Kylian Mbappé 2020 (*Sorare*)
- $63,000 – Bruno Fernandes 2019-20 (*Sorare*)
- $60,000 – 'Hyperion' (*Gods Unchained*)

(USD, at time of purchase)

Fig 4.12 Most Expensive Game NFTs

However, you can't just create any NFTs within these platforms and expect to sell them for a high price. But you can follow the method of gaining traction.

Let's look at the example of NBA Top Shot. A lot of NFTs on this platform are costly at the moment. You may see the Lebron James' NFTs are selling for more than $250,000. Of course, we're too late. However, we can use this method for newer NFTs that are not at a high price yet. If we go back into the history of the NFT, let's say we were early in the space. We can see the first sale price was $1,200, and then shortly after it was sold for $1,600, it was sold for $2,000 later. So we can see that it would be around this time that this thing is gaining traction. We weren't the first person to buy, but after a few of these sales, we can see that people are actually buying it, and it is gaining traction. That's where we want to enter. Of course, some of these prices might be too high for some people, but this is the truth about NFTs. It's a game where you pay to play. There's a misconception that NFT is just you jump in and create, and boom, you become rich. However, that's not how it works. The only time that works is if you are the person of influence and have a platform to market. Unfortunately, if you are not that person, you will have to pay to play if you want to get your hands on one of these valuable NFTs.

If we check other NBA NFTs, we can also find some NFTs are at lower prices currently, like $2 or even $1. If you see they're getting higher bids, like $4 or $6, we know they're getting tractions, and people are willing to buy it, which is the time we want to go into one of these NFTs.

This also can be applied on any platforms like OpenSea and Rarible. Every time you're looking at an NFT, it will show the history, what people were bidding, and what people were paying for. If you're getting in early enough and paying attention, and you see that one NFT was sold for $50 and $100, then $200, which means it's gaining attention and traction, and that would be your entry point.

2. Either creating NFTs being an influencer or buying NFTs from a person of influence

Let's look at the following example:

This is the NFT called EthBoy, created by Trevor Jones, and was sold for 260 ETH, approximately $141,704 at that time. You might be wondering why someone would pay so much for this digital piece of art. The artist Trevor Jones has built up a reputation in the NFT artworks, so people are pretty much buying the reputation when he creates a painting. Also, when you have influence, your platform is excellent for instant marketing.

Another example is Justin Roiland, his Rick and Morty has been sold for over $1 Million in Ether. As soon as he creates a piece of art, people know about it, and they trust his reputation. This is something that we see in the regular art world. People aren't necessarily paying for what's on the paper, and people are paying for the artist. The same thing is happening here in the NFT art world, but not all of you listening are a person of influence or have a platform.

As introduced before, **Nifty Gateway** is best for exclusive drops. On Nifty, you can find Justin Roiland's collection and his coming releasing plans. When you check, you may find that most of the old ones have been sold out, which brings an important concept of NFTs. They are non-fungible tokens, and they are rare. Sometimes there's only one piece available, and sometimes there are only five or ten available prints. You need to understand that investing in NFTs is much different than investing in regular cryptocurrency. If someone does all the research for a cryptocurrency project, and they say go ahead and buy it. You can go ahead and copy their trades but remember these NFTs are limited. If there's only one of one, or ten of ten, someone can't do all the research, and then say all right, go ahead copy my trade and buy it, because they just have to buy it from you. So for you, instead of learning what to buy, it's much more important to know how to buy with these methods.

If you are the person of influence or you don't have a platform, the method for you will be gaining traction from a person of influence. For example, if Logan Paul was going to release a limited edition of his NFT artwork, and you are aware of him, and you follow his social media, you will know earlier than others that he is going to release an NFT. One of the biggest risks of buying an NFT is that you may purchase an NFT that no one else wants. You might get it for a low price, but you may not be able to resell it after. Now, gaining traction from influencers can help you reduce your risks.

Let's say Logan Paul released an NFT. Someone buys it for $100, and then right after someone buys it for $150, and then right after $200. You can see that it's gaining traction, and this may be a good entry point to get in and buy it. You can tell that there is a trend that people are willing to pay more for it. But if you go in too early, you might just buy something that no one else wants.

So If we aren't the people of influence ourselves, we can follow those people of influence, and we can gain traction. Sometimes you could become the person of influence in the crypto art world. Christie's auction house sells NFT artworks from famous digital artist Beeple, a man named Mike Winkelmann from Wisconsin. He is a regular person who has created his own influence and reputation within this digital world. So it is possible you can create random arts on Rarible, and maybe one day you will become this person, and your works will sell. But the likelihood is very low. It is a higher probability that you will be able to sell NFT artwork of value if you purchase it from someone who already has built that reputation.

3. Try to buy the first

This means that the first NFT from the specific creator or its first kind in the industry has the best value. That's why the CryptoKitties are so valuable now since they were the first ones ever created. They will always have some significant values because people love that. The first NFT from the creator is historical. The first ones always create buzz, excitement, and hype. So if you can buy into something that is first, chances are it will be valued by fans of that artist, brand, or genre.

4. Tangible ones can have more values

This means that NFT should have some tangible elements, like physical assets behind it or experience. For example, for Logan Paul's NFT, you will have a chance to meet him if you have his NFTs.

5. Domain names

If we go on to OpenSea, we can see that some of these domain names have already sold for a high price. Something to notice here is that they're all very short names, like "wallet.eth", "google.eth", and "amazon.eth", etc. We learned from the previous domain bubble that people are willing to pay a lot of money for a valuable domain. The short ".com" ones have been sold for millions of dollars: business.com is worth 345 million dollars,carinsurance.com is worth 49 million dollars.

For the domain name NFTs, it's best to buy something with one word, sometimes you can get by with two words, but three-word domain names likely won't be valuable in the future. You also need to pay attention to the ending of the domain names, and there are ".eth," ".crypto," etc. In the traditional domain name world, the ones ending with ".com" are more valuable than others, ending with".net."

So the gamble that you're making here is guessing which one of these domain names will be the winner in 20 years, whether the winner will be ".eth," ".crypto," or something else. Suppose you want a very valuable domain that is one word, something like "wallet.eth", unfortunately, you will have to go to the open marketplace and pay a premium for it. Or you can start from scratch. You can go to **Ens domains** to buy ".eth," or you can go to **unstoppable domains** to buy ".crypto" or others. The downside here is that you're going to have a tough time getting your hands on very simple domain names that are the more premium ones and have already been bought, and you will have to get them on an open marketplace.

6. Scarcity is key

This one is easy to understand. The more rare something is, the more valuable it will be.

4.6 Which NFT Industries Worth Most Of Your Attention Now
1. Sports NFTs

This is one of the best NFT applications, and we will see a massive amount of growth. The most famous example is NBA Top Shot. The sports NFTs is likely to change the history of the sport, not only for the investors and the average avid collectors who collect the cards, but more importantly for the players themselves who will be able to negotiate into their contracts rights over the footage of themselves playing the sports that they can then create into an NFT and sell it to their biggest fans. This will be a new way to monetizing sports which is huge. Imagine Michael Phelps creates an NFT of himself finishing first and getting all his gold medals at the Olympics. The moments people have fallen in love with throughout sports history may worth a couple hundred of thousands of dollars, but in the future, this can get even crazier when technologies catch up and make it easier for people actually to get into this and invest instead of having to watch a long video.

2. EDM Music Industry

Musician 3LAU has sold the world's first-ever crypto-albums and made $11.6 million within 24 hours. For these EDM musicians, they can generate hype, and the EMD industry is massive. The kinds of fans that belong to it are the best fans you can imagine because they're incredibly loyal and will go out of the way to support their favorite music artists. This is a niche that is set for massive growth and worths your attention.

4.7 What's the Disadvantage Of Trading NFTs

One disadvantage of trading NFTs is it's very challenging to copy or follow another trader's trades. With a stock or a cryptocurrency, if someone breaks it down and explains its technical analysis and they buy it. You might agree with them, and you might go ahead and buy it as well. But with NFTs, you cannot copy someone else's trade. NFTs are rare and unique. So if someone buys an NFT, it's no longer available for you to buy it. So this space is tricky and not as easy as people might think. But maybe you have some knowledge or advice on a certain subcategory. Perhaps a certain niche within the art world or a certain niche within the gaming world will do well.

4.8 Are There Risks and Scams To Be Aware Of?

There are scams even on the most reputable marketplaces. The best way to avoid this is to purchase from those verified sellers. Trading NFTs as trading in the stock market. If you are not experienced, make sure you are not spending more than you can or be willing to lose.

We will talk more about the risks of trading NFTS in the later chapter.

Chapter 5

NFT Selling, Trading & Swapping

What you have learned and/or have done so far:

1. understand what an NFT is.
2. Select an NFT trading platform
3. Connect it with your Crypto wallet
4. Create or/and Buy your NFTs.

Now the question is: how to sell my NFTs? After going through the previous chapters, you are probably not looking for the step-by-step instructions on how to list your NFTs and click the sell button. You're more likely to want to know some practical strategies about how to make sales on the NFTs you created and how to price the NFTs you collected to make the most profits out of them. So let's talk about these in this chapter.

5.1 As NFT Creators or Artists, How to Make Sales

It is essential that you are using one or all of the following platforms:

- Twitter
- Facebook Groups
- Discord
- Reddit

The more you use, the better. Many people think about selling their NFTs the wrong way. They believe that if they can get into a large platform, somehow, they're going to get all the eyes, attention, views, and buyers to take their works. However, this is actually wrong. You have to build a connection with the community, get to know the people better, and then the art collectors are going to notice you.

Currently, a lot of people are just spamming their works on Twitter whenever there's an artist. They haunt and dm them," look at me, check out my artworks." But if you do that, you're just going to annoy the collectors, and the art collectors are not going to buy from you. Some collectors even have tweeted that to stop ding and messaging him about the works. If your artwork is good, he's going to notice you. The key is that don't annoy the art collectors.

Instead, you can follow different NFT art collectors and vendors on Twitter. You don't need to bug them, but you can participate in the conversations. You can comment on their works, share their works, and use hashtags.

Each platform has its own discord. If you scroll to the very bottom of these NFT platforms, like Nifty Gateway, they have a discord link at the very bottom that you can join those communities. You can talk to people, check their works. These discord groups usually have a channel where you can post your works, whether it's digital art, photography, or other NFT works that you are trying to sell, hopefully. Don't go spamming people all the time. What you should do is trying to engage with the community and get to know people. People will begin to notice you, and these art collectors hang out in these kinds of places. They maybe don't say much, but they're there.

You can also go to Reddit. On Reddit, there are communities where creators and artists can post their work. So collectors will see these works. Just post your works, and also be sure to check out other people's comments on them. If you're on Facebook, you can share your work on Facebook pages or groups. Make sure when you share your artworks, also befriend people, make connections. They get to know you after a while. These people are going to start retweeting and sharing your works too.

If you an Apple user, you can also consider Clubhouse. There are always some NFT rooms open or Clubhouse meetings. If you're patient enough, you can talk and lead people to check out your work when it comes down to your turn. Collectors also hang out there too.

These sound like a lot of work out there, but it shouldn't be a chore for you to make friends with other people, engage with other creators, and discover new work. If you're really an artist and really into it for the long run, then you're going to enjoy this process. But if you're just someone in it for the money and don't want to go through all digital artworks, then maybe being an NFT artist is not for you. This is not the industry to make quick money out of it, and this is something that you should really enjoy doing.

Another helpful site that's worth mentioning here is tryshowtime.com. It will display all the artworks you created, listed, and sold. This can help if you use Linktree; you can have one link that shows all of your NFTs and crypto arts. People can access your artwork very easily across multiple platforms.

Extra hacks on selling

1. Some artists tend to set their work at a very low price, like $1 or $2. However, if you price it too low, you would not make back the money you spent on it. So don't sell yourself short.
2. During the selling process, you will collect the different coins from selling NFTs. You may not want to transfer them into Etherum right away because you will need to pay the transfer fee every time you do the transfer, which means you will lose money. Instead, you want to build up a little and do one transfer.
3. Suppose you choose the platforms that do need you to pay the gas fee. You can check Gasnow.org, which will provide you the updated information on the gas fee, so you can choose to list and sell your NFTs when the gas fee is at the lowest.

5.2 As NFT collectors, How to Value NFTs

More and more people are beginning to collect NFTs. Since there are many categories of NFTs and a wide range of different NFTs, it's almost impossible to tell you at what price you should buy and re-sell your NFT collections. But if you know how to value these unique digital assets accurately, you will be able to manage your NFT collection like a pro and make the most profit from them as you can.

5.2.1 Ways to Value NFTs

There are **objective** and **subjective** dimensions to value NFTs.

People might consider the low-trait CryptoPunk they claimed for free back in 2017 is priceless. But these kinds of basic punks have been traded regularly on NFT marketplaces, which lead to their **objective floor prices** naturally develop over time. Let's look at the CryptoPunks, and the price floor is around 19 ETH at the time of writing, which means if you list your CryptoPunk at this price level, you have a good chance to sell it quickly as many buyers keep tracking the most affordable prices.

When do the objective valuations, you need to consider **rare traits** if possible and whether the projects have **hard-coded primary sale prices**. For example, a common Avastar is usually started with 0.07 ETH, and the uncommon one is always 0.14 ETH.

Another critical dimension to consider is **time**. It is what did the NFT worth in the past time? What's its value currently, and what can it be worth years later? How has the value changed over time, was it change rapidly or slowly? If you can dig into these questions, you will be able to valuate any NFTs better.

Recently, there's another dimension we need to consider simultaneously is the **analytic** dimension. Estimate and analyze a neutral, conservative, and aggressive NFT valuation on a rolling basis. Being able to do this will give you a framework to understand and approach all the implications of "ifs," including what if the NFT cools down, what if its market heats up, what if it stays flat?

For example, if you own a CrypKitties Founder cat, you want to evaluate its value next year. If the NFT bull market can continue over the coming months, your aggressive analysis may be that your Kitty worth dozens of ETH. But your conservative analysis is likely that you can get whatever the floor price of the Founder cat is if the NFT's bear market comes and you want to sell.

These are the common ways of how people approach understanding the valuation of NFTs. The better way to accurately value the NFT is to weigh its reigning market conditions against its objective and fundamental elements.

Now, it's time to walk through the most critical value-additive elements.

5.2.2 Seven Traits that Drive the value of NFTs

1. On-chains

Most NFTs are minted on-chain and rely on Ethereum smart contracts to exist. This is to say they can last as long as Ethereum exists, which is very likely to be a very long time. Some NFT projects choose to ease by making their NFTs on external off-chain providers like AWS. This will need more trust, and you need to hope that this project can last and keep the server running. You are at risk of owning a blank NFT in the next few years.

So, the more on-chain the NFT is, the more raw self-evident value it has since it's able to prove itself and can do it anytime.

Two Key questions for off-chain vs. on-chain:

- Where is the NFT hosted?
- Is the NFT fully on-chain?

2. Chain security

As long as the underlying blockchain infrastructure stays guaranteed and immutable, the NFTs will be guaranteed and immutable digital assets. Ethereum is one of the most secured smart contract platforms running now, and this dominance is foreseen to be continued in the future. This is why NFTs created on Ethereum are now more valuable than those minted elsewhere. They're just more secure.

Two key questions on-chain security:

- Is it sufficiently decentralized?
- Is the host chain secure?

3. Age

NFTs' value also depends on when they were created. For instance, NFTs began to heat up in 2020, and NFTs that precede this era is starting to take off, similar to the earliest pieces in the cultural revolution. While we are still at the early stage, we cannot say the age factor is settled yet. It's possible that any NFTs minted before 2050 still has excellent potential.

The earliest NFT projects like the CryptoPunks are already with significant valuations. So similar to wine, keep age in mind, always!

Two key questions on age:

- Is there any historical relevance to this NFT?
- When was this NFT created or minted?

4. Scarcity

In this ecosystem, some creators released NFTs as 1 of 1, and others will do multi-editions like 1 of 50s or 1 of 100s, etc. It's obvious that 1 of 1 is hyper-scarce and can be super valuable on the foundational level compared to those diluted with multiple editions. But this doesn't mean the multi-edition NFTs cannot be valuable. Some of them have reached for thousands of dollars too. If you're shopping for rare 1 of 1 NFTs, go to platforms like SuperRare, which only supports 1 of 1 edition.

Two key questions on scarcity:

- How many pieces were created?
- Will the artist keep their social contracts and won't create more prints?

5. Artists & Communities

If the artists or creators are with no followers and no history of creating NFT drops, will their work sell? Probably not without extra efforts. The NFTs published by major creators or popular artists will naturally have more value. Similarly, engaging communities will also create demand and more exposure to potential buyers.

The more popular the artists or creators, the bigger the communities, the more valuable the NFTs will be. Actually, this also applies to other markets too.

Three questions on artists & communities:

- Do the artists or creators have followers on social platforms like Instagram and Twitter?
- Do you think the artists will grow their brand in the future?
- Do the artists interact with their fans often?

6. Release Pace

Did the creator create 10 1 of 1 NFTs in a year or 1,000 NFTs? Figuring out the artist's production pace is also vital for understanding their NFTs' value.

The projects that provide 1,000 or even more NFTs are generally less appealing compared to purchasing an NFT from the artists who are committed to only creating 20 NFTs ever. This is similar to the scarcity element. Naturally, famous artists that only release a selected few NFT artworks each year sell for higher than similar-niche artists who release multiple pieces every week.

One unique scenario is the artist Beeple who sold his entire collection with 5,000 pieces for around $70 million. He created one piece every day for over 13 years, and it took over a decade of persistent work to build up that level of reputation and valuation, though.

Two key questions on release pace:

- How many pieces of artwork have these artists created?
- At what pace is this artist creating new work? (is it daily, weekly, monthly, annually?)

7. Richness

Now more and more visual NFTs are created with accompanying audio. We're seeing this dynamic provides NFT collectors a richer artistic experience than the plain traditional NFTs. Who won't like music playing as their NFT goes on that oddly satisfying loop?

The audio can boost the NFTs' value with the sensual addiction, and particularly the audio is completed in collaboration with popular artists. We can expect this visual-audio edition to become a new artistic norm in the near future.

Two key questions on richness:

- Is the NFT with audio?

- Who participated in creating the audio for this NFT?

Bonus: Rarity of Project-Specific

There are some NFT projects, including Axie Infinity and CryptoPunks, that have their special traits. For example, to CryptoPunks, alien and ape punks are a lot more valuable than the standard punk. The Mystic Axies are the rarest and most valuable ones on the Axies market.

Basically, the rarer their traits, the more profits you can expect from them. Next time, if you see a big NFT sale, but feel confused about it, try to dig into their underlying traits.

The Bottom Line

When it comes to valuing NFTs, there are no absolute right or wrong answers. When you try to evaluate NFTs, consider the dynamics and factors mentioned above. Your best bet is to take the holistic approach and understand all the projects' aspects before pulling the trigger.

Have you heard of the MoonCats project? They were released just after CryptoPunks but went dark after 2017. However, now the NFT ecosystem just rediscovered them. Recently, hundreds of people have created MoonCats and tried to value them on the NFT market - OpenSea.

So what's the truth?

Investors are still trying to figure out how to value them accurately, and no standard answer yet. We probably will value them differently now compared to 1, 5, or 10 years later.

But keep in mind the fundamentals: Is the NFT on-chain? Is its creator reputable? Does the artist engage in the community? Any unique underlying traits?

Ask yourself these basic questions when you invest NFTs. The trick is to take everything you know and every information you can gather about the NFT into consideration.

You need to tackle evaluating and valuing NFTs from multiple angles. However, if you can, you're way ahead of this curve.

5.3 NFT Trading & Swapping

One of the most painful problems that NFT collectors are facing is the lack of liquidity for NFTs. How many times were there no right buyers or sellers on the other side? Fortunately, there are some platforms available trying to help with this issue.

- **NFT20**

What is NFT20?

NFT20 is a permissionless protocol for tokenizing NFTs and making them tradable on decentralized exchanges like UniSwap. This enables anyone to create an NFT contract pool and gett ERC20 token derivatives of their NFTs in a permissionless way. These tokens can be transferred and traded on DEXes immediately. $Muse is the governance token of NFT20, and you are able to farm $Muse by providing liquidity to different NFT20 token pairs. You can use $Muse for specific votes on NFT20to burn and get fees the DEX generates and act as a hedge for the NFT market. Also, you can sell $Muse on uniswap.

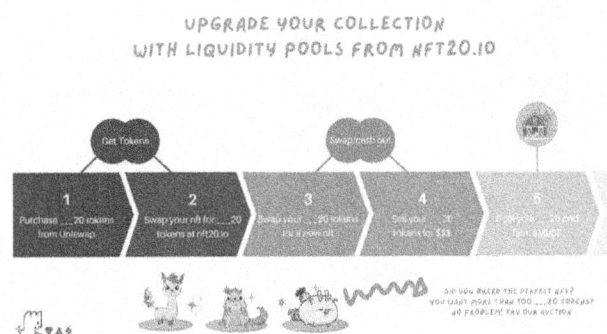

Fig 6.1 NFT20 (Source:NFT20.IO)

How can NFT20 help the NFT holders?

If there's a pool available for your NFTs, for every NFT deposited in it, the contract generates 100 ERC20 tokens belong to this NFT project. For these 100 tokens, you will get 95 tokens, and the leftover 5 tokens will be the DEX fee that will get distributed equally to $Muse token holders.

You can use those tokens in several ways immediately, including:

1. Swap the tokens that you have received for another NFT available in the pool. This swapping NFTs for NFTs in a permissionless way.

2. Sell the tokens on Uniswap for profit if you have enough liquidity.
3. Use the tokens to bid on auctions for higher quality NFTs. For instance, you can tokenize ten crypto kitties and one thousand tokens. You can use these tokens to buy a gen 0 kitty if it's available for auction.

- **What if you don't want to tokenize your NFT to swap it for other NFTs in the same pool?**

You can simply toggle the "swap NFT to NFT" at the top right of the pool.

- **What if your NFT is worth more than 100 tokens?**

If you think your NFT worths more than 100 tokens, you can choose to create a Dutch auction and set up your ideal price, and you can cancel it anytime you want. The bids and final payment will be in the pool's token.

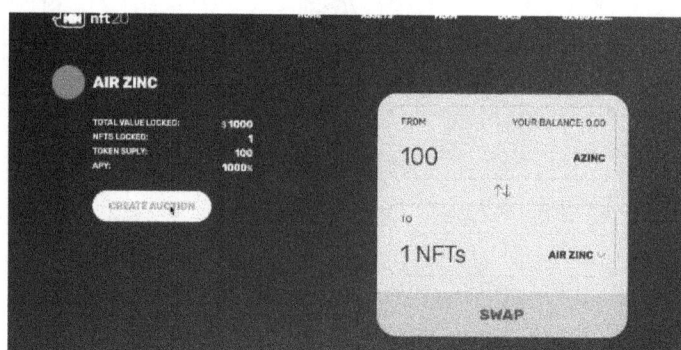

Fig 6.2 Create Auction on NFT20

How can NFT20 help NFT projects' founders?

After the project's founders create a pool for their project, the NFT20 factory will create a new contract with a new token. If you have enough liquidity on Uniswap, you will have a better idea of the new speculators in your project since they can have liquidity for their NFTs anytime. The project owners can also get 5% of all auctions sold within NFT20.

Having a healthy pool on a DEX with good liquidity enables your users to trade NFTs easily. Newcomers can get their NFTs at a fair price too. NFT project developers can use the pool as a sale mechanism and the pair to get high liquidity.

Your project's users will be able to buy and sell their NFTs in a more flexible and liquid way; also, arbitrage opportunities can be created on second-hand markets like OpenSea where you can capture fees.

Another further step you can do as the project founder is to incentivize your users to add liquidity and trade the newly created tokenized version of your NFTs. The projects with high liquidity will be incentive to received governance tokens from NFT20 at launch. In order to incentive LP taking, you can use the already made contract or standers like the following example:

<u>Sushi swap's MasterChef</u>

How to create a pool?

Creating a pool is not as hard as you might think. It's giving your NFT token address and sending the transactions. It will help your community achieve liquidity and swaps for all your NFTs in a more straightforward way. ERC721 and ERC1155 are the current ones to support NFTs.

1. Go to <u>https://nft20.io/assets</u>.
2. Click on "**ADD ASSET.**"
3. Please paste in the NFT address and click "**CREATE NFT EXCHANGE.**"
4. Pay the Transaction fees.

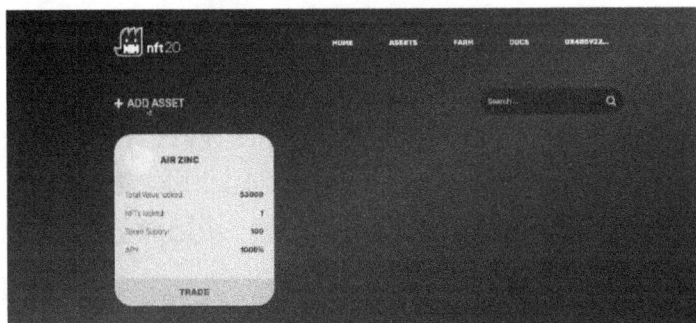

Fig 6.3 Add Asset on NFT20

That's it! It's done! Now you can visit your asset page on NFT20 and tokenize any of your NFTs for you and your community.

Use with Caution

NFT20 is still at its very early stage, and their contracts were NOT audited. So please use it with caution and don't put into more than what you are willing to lose if hacks happen.

- **BoxSwap**

BoxSwap is another platform allowing users to swap NFTs. Its wallet feature enables users to view and manage their portfolios. It's based on 0x that is a protocol for the decentralized exchange of ERC721 and ERC20. So liquidity for ERC20 tokens is offered by 0x relayers, and the transactions are peer to peer.

How to use BoxSwap for swapping NFTS?

BoxSwap's interface is clean and user-friendly.

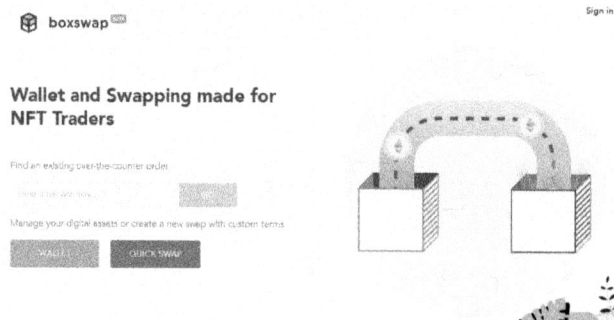

Fig 6.4 Boxswap

Step 1: Install **MetaMask wallet** and log in.

Step 2: Navigate to **BoxSwap**, and you will see the notification from MetaMaks for connecting requests. Accept it and click "Quick Swap" to create your order.

Step 3: Swap. For example, if you have one crypto kittie and want to swap for an Axie of Axie Infinity. You can choose the Kitty you would like to send and write Axie's TokenID in return and add that Axie's owner's address.

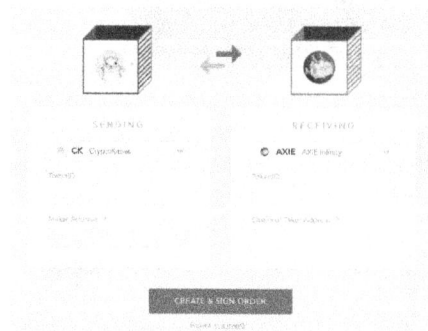

Fig 6.5 NFT swapping on Boxswap

If you don't have another NFT that you want to swap for, it's ok too. You can create an order to sell your crypto kitty for ERC20 tokens without specifying any taker address. Anyone can fill your order within your order's duration.

Step 4: Once you set the terms, create and sign orders, you can see a page that you can share with whether the owner of the address you entered or anyone if the taker's address is left blank in order to fill the order.

BoxSwap can help you swap NFTs easily and efficiently. It also provides a discord server where has BoxSwap's SwapBot. Axie Infinity supports it, and you are able to create a swap directly using a simple command.

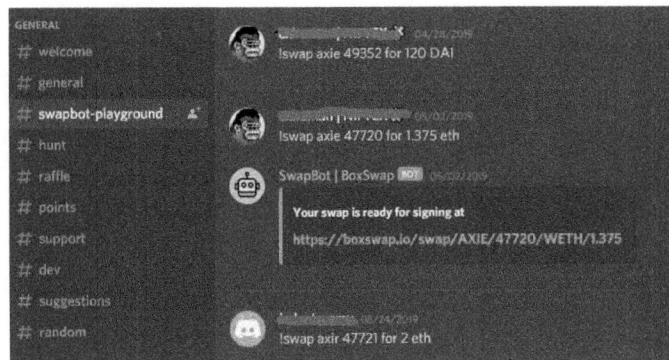

Fig 6.6 Boxswap discord

As shown in the above pictures, users use "!swap" to create the swap directly. If you need more information or instruction, you can use the command "!help".

Also, you can use BoxSwap to buy ERC20 tokens. It's also a wallet where you can check your cryptocurrencies and NFT assets with its excellent UI design.

Currently, BoxSwap supports swap between the following:

- Axies of Axie Infinity
- Block of BlockCities
- CryptoKitties
- WrappedKitties (WCK)
- CSC
- Dai Stablecoin (DAI)
- Donut
- Flower of Flowerpatch
- Luna
- LAND of Decentraland

- MANA of Decentraland
- Maker (MKR)
- MLBCB – cryptobaseball
- NEO – NeoDistrict
- REP -Reputation
- WETH – Wrapped Ether
- ZRX – 0x

MetaMak

Recently, Metamask provides the swapping feature for both its web and mobile version allowing users to swap one token for another.

If you want to swap, open Metamask, tap the new "Swap" button where you will be able to choose the tokens you want to exchange, choose a quote, and swipe to do the swap. You can also see the estimated fees for the swap above the "Swipe to swap" button.

MetaMask uses multiple automated market makers (AMMs) and decentralized exchanges (DEXs) in order to find the best price for that particular token. According to them, their calculations of gas prices will lead to decreased gas costs too. Besides, MetaMask spread orders across various exchanges to lower slippage costs by employing slippage protection.

Now you can download the apps for free on **MetaMask's website**.

5.4 Environmental Impacts of NFT Trading

Many stories are circulating regarding the blockchain legers' high energy usage – Bitcoin mining uses a similar quantity of electricity as Denmark annually. This is a problem, while it's not down to NFT trading itself, rather their underlying blockchains' security processes.

To add a new block to the blockchain, specific numbers have to be mined and verified, which consumes a large amount of computing power but makes creating false information in blocks very hard too. Besides, in order to edit a block, each block after it needs to be edited correctly as well.

The blockchain ecosystem does not ignore this issue. Ethereum is now rolling out a new model using financial stakes instead of massive computing tasks to validate new blocks. ETH2, the new version of Ethereum, works the same as the previous model in every other way but can facilitate NFT trading transparently and securely and decrease its environmental impact. It predicts to decrease 99.98% of the energy consumed, and this energy-saving potential is huge for the ecosystem.

You might think this could remove the decentralization of blockchain, but it won't. It's just a different approach for nodes across the network to stay secured. ETH2 is expected to improve efficiency without waiting for a new block to be mined in order to add a transaction.

Chapter 6

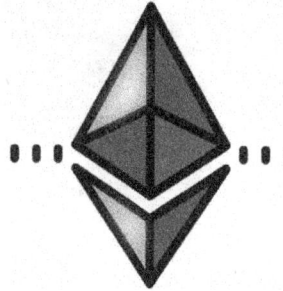

Let's Delve Into NFT Use Cases

Theoretically speaking, the NFTs' scope is anything unique that needs provable ownership. NFTs are gaining traction, and the use cases are only going to increase in number. This rise in popularity also will open a wide range of possibilities for virtual and real-world assets. Even right now, NFTs have come in very handy in many different use cases. Their ability to easily verify originality and scarcity of digital information cannot be taken lightly. Let's delve into the current and big NFT use cases. As an NFT investor, which NFT use case captures your interest most? What value can it provide you?

6.1 NFT Use Case #1

Digital Art

Digital artists can have a nightmare protecting their creations against copyright infringement, and it can be difficult for those talented creators to make a living. But NFTs provide a solution as they can offer proof of authenticity and ownership by blockchain to eliminate fraud and counterfeiting issues. The buyers can show the artwork in the digital space, being fully aware of the history of the art assets, including date of creation, artist's name, list of previous owners, and asset's values throughout its lifecycle. Artists can also get better payment for their artwork by initiating P2P payments and eliminating the brokers.

According to CoinDesk, as galleries and museums are forced to close under the Covid-19 pandemic, many artists have turned into NFTs and online showrooms. As they noted, "Just as Bitcoin has paved the way for peer-to-peer, trusting transactions by creating a shared events ledger, the crypto art has provenance built-in."

The most common type of NFT art available now is programmable art, a blend of creativity and technology. Many limited editions can be programmed to change upon various circumstances being met. Artists can use smart contracts and oracles to create images that respond to the crypto assets' variation.

The first sale record for the high-valued NFT auction was in July 2020: The "Picasso's Bull" was sold for over $55,000. Subsequent records include "Right Place & Right Time," which was purchased over $100,000, and "Portraits of a Mind," sold for more than $130,000. Cointelegraph points out that those art projects can even streamline and improve artists' revenue by connecting them directly to potential buyers through exchange solutions and blockchain-based payment.

On the other hand, platforms and marketplaces for digital art like SuperRare, OpenSea, and Rarible allow users to make original digital artworks and sell them easily. For example, Rarible brought together some of the more interesting 2020 DeFi trends by combining digital collectibles with liquidity mining and yield farming. Rarible accomplished this by issuing their governance token - $RARI, which became one of the reasons for the renewed interest in NFTs happened in the last few months of 2020. When users trade and sell their NFTs on the platform, they can get incentivized and rewarded with $RARI. Rarible is becoming a fully Decentralized community-governed marketplace in this way. Other platforms also started issuing and distributing their governance tokens, like Somnium Space ($CUBES), Sandbox ($SAND), and Decentraland ($MANA).

The legacy arts industry is also applying blockchain technology by tokenizing real-world artworks and assets. This comes as a combination of Blockchain and IoT, which provides people the ability to scan the codes on stickers placed on the back of the paintings and register as the piece's owner on the blockchain.

6.2 NFT Use Case #2

Collectibles

Collectibles is one of the first ways people learn how to apply NFTs and currently one of the most popular NFT applications in terms of sales volume, with around 23.6% of the sales coming from collectible-related projects.

In June 2017, **CryptoPunks** was one of the first NFT collectibles on Ethereum and sold for hundreds of thousands of dollars.

The much-loved **CryptoKitties** their popularity congested the Ethereum network at the peak in 2017 and is still one of the most notorious collectible examples. CryptoKitties are unique digital kittens that can be bred to create more unique ones with more favorable specific characteristics than others (like the fur pattern or eye color). The sales for the kittens have achieved an all-time volume of more than $38 million.

The latest NFT collectible many people are chasing is **Good Morning Crypto**, and the most popular ones are Ivan on Tech, Big Boy Pants. The limited editions include "Big Strong Guy" and the Halloween "Big Boy Pumpkin Pants."

This NFT category will continue to expand and develop as NFT technology is being leveraged to make tokenized versions of star celebrities and athletes for their fans to collect. The Sorare, a fantasy soccer game, allows its users to collect limited edition digital collectibles of their favorite athletes among 100 football clubs.

Members of the NBA and NFL showed their interest in collaborating with NFT technology during the NFT NYC in Feb 2020. Since then, the CryptoKitties creators Dapper Labs partnered with NBA and launched **NBA TopShot**. Caty Tedman, the Dapper Lab's head of partnerships and marketing, said, "NBA TopShot is meant to offer fans a piece of ownership over the actions that happened on the court."

After tapping into the bases of passionate fans, NFT collectibles have shown their power and potential to bring these communities to the blockchain. More traditional collections were dragged into blockchain technology by NFTs, including **coins, trading cards, and stamps**.

Terra Virtua, a digital collectible platform, stands out at the forefront of the NFT collectibles movements. It takes digital collectibles in a multiplatform

AR and VR world, aiming to offer users a "deep sensory experience." Terra Virtua launched a character-based 3D animated collection named "vFlects" together with licensed collectibles in 2D and 3D from Top Gun, the Godfather, Sunset Boulevard and Lost in Space. They not only provide a marketplace for the interactive range of licensed and unique digital collectibles but an ecosystem through their Terra Virtua Fracave and art gallery app enabling the cross-platform journey. In the art gallery app, users can display, store, and interact with and show off their collections of unique NFTs. On the other side, the Terra Virtua Francave is a customizable and personalized VR environment where owners can display the collections. The CEO at Terra Virtua, Gary Bracey, stated, "Terra Virtua's key mission is to bring NFTs to the big market. The core videogame experience offers a strong focus on UI and UX by providing a compelling and frictionless process. We hope to bring the interactive digital collectibles world to the mainstream. " Terra Virtua provides its users the cross-platform capabilities and sensory element, which pushes NFTs to the next level as products into truly interactive and engaging experiences.

6.3 NFT Use Case #3

Game Industry

The gaming industry was a natural fit for NFTs. Virtual economies have existed in the game's ecosystem for years and have been the staples in games like the World of Warcraft and Fortnite. Currencies, in-game collectibles, and marketplaces are the focus of these games, leveraging which the gamers progress and level up through the games.

The prominent game accounts that excelled through the games are a hot commodity for those who are unwilling to spend time and effort to unlock the bonus features. Due to this, there is quite an underground market for such accounts, which goes largely unregulated.

Blockchain-based gaming allows players to trade in-game assets securely while offering a layer of validation and authenticity. In addition, it facilitates the rare items openly for fiat money securely and safely. NFTs provide an excellent solution for digital ownership of rare and unique in-game collectibles, allowing users to generate real-world revenue by leveraging their gaming skills.

Users can also participate in the governance to decide the direction of future developments in a game. This provides users the opportunity to design their virtual work, operating the same within digitally verifiable in-game marketplaces.

In-game items can be tokenized and exchanged or transferred easily with peer-to-peer marketplaces and trading, which is not like traditional ones that prohibit the transfer or sale of gaming assets, including rare skins and weapons. Thanks to NFTs, the gaming experience becomes more rewarding and tangible since players now have true ownership over their virtual assets. Besides, players are even able to earn money by creating and developing their in-game assets, which create a new economy.

The blockchain's critical potential is the theory that the loyalty of players will increase when having more skins and other assets in the game: If their virtual assets can be transferred between platforms or games or traded on open markets, they will be willing to invest more of their hard-earned cash, according to Cointelegraph.

A Galaxy Interactive pamphlet demonstrates that digital goods can earn the same status as their physical counterparts. What we created inside of our virtual worlds, their values will become more indistinguishable from the value we have historically made outside of them.

Creating virtual economies fuelled by gaming NFTs opened the way to a new gaming ecosystem that was never possible before. This incorporation encourages developing an interactive and engaging community since players start to build an inherent community by peer-to-peer trading.

<u>Axie Infinity</u>, <u>My crypto Heroes</u>, and <u>Gods Unchained</u> are the three popular blockchain games that have taken off.

Axie Infinity is a virtual pet community focused on raising, collecting, training, and battling fantasy creatures called Axie. It's built on the Ethereum blockchain and is the first blockchain-based on feature animated characters and immersive gameplay.

Gods Unchained is a virtual collectible card game. Game cards are issued as NFTs, and players can trade also own them with the same level of ownership as physical ones.

My Crypto Heroes is a multiplayer role-playing battle game from Japan. It issues heroes and gaming items as tokens on the Ethereum blockchain, where players are capable of leveling up historical heroes through tournaments and quests.

6.4 NFT Use Case #4

Real Estate or Virtual Worlds

Real estate seems to be the most interesting tokenization project, where the property is getting tokenized on the blockchain. There is no better way to do this than by NFTs. A single property can be fractionalized into multiple assets that allowing to be bought by investors on the blockchain exchange, enabling people to claim the ownership of that property. Tokenizing the real estate allow smoother and more liquid transaction as one person is buying or selling the house ensuring fraud prevention and transparency. By eliminating any third-party intermediary, it can prevent any conflict over the estate or land ownership.

Decentralized virtual reality marketplaces like **Crytovoxels**, **Decentraland**, the **Sandbox** allow users to own, create and monetize parcels of virtual land and other in-game assets. Decentraland's LAND is owned by the community permanently and offers players complete control over their virtual assets and creations.

Assets in virtual worlds give the public flexibility and options that align with the next generation's values. Our children may not own the roof over their heads; however, they will own a wealth of virtual assets instead.

6.5 NFT Use Case #5

Music

Music can be linked with NFTs too. Only the person who indeed claims the file's ownership can access it. **Mintbase** and **Rarible** are two marketplaces and platforms allowing musicians to create their songs into NFTs.

When we look at this from music listeners' perspectives, only a limited number of these records will be available since they cannot be distributed and duplicated. This provides a sense of exclusivity to listeners. Featuring the music a collectible-quality is similar to that of vinyl, but modern technology provides the possibility for this awesomeness.

In pre-digital popular culture, a music record collection was one of the most common forms of collectibles. However, this was overturned by the introduction of music streaming sites and the internet. Music pirating gets rife and costs musicians millions. NFT approach benefits musicians a lot by providing them the opportunity to eliminate the middlemen and reach out to their fans directly.

6.6 NFT Use Case #6

Fashion

NFT has blended with the fashion industry seamlessly and offers benefits to all people who participated in the supply chain. For consumers, they can now digitally verify the ownership of all their items and accessories to eliminate the counterfeiting risk. Simply scan a QR code on the sale tag attached to the internal label as an NFT. Consumers also are able to know the details like date and the place of creation of the asset, previous owners, etc. Applying blockchain to the fashion industry can also help increase employee welfare, reduce the level of carbon dioxide emission, and protect customers.

6.7 NFT Use Case #7

Sports and Event Tickets

The sports industry suffered a lot due to forgery and mass ticket hoarding, as well as counterfeit merchandise. The blockchain can help eliminate these. With NFTs, the game tickets can be authenticated and verified on the blockchain without a practical way of cheating the system, thanks to the records' immutability kept on the distributed ledger. Each event ticket may be similar. However, each one will have unique identifiable information of the designated owner on the blockchain. Besides, in order to prevent mass hoarding, tickets can be bound to a specific blockchain-based identity to enforce selling limits.

Sports NFTs are gaining recent popularity with those prominent athletes becoming tokenized assets on the blockchain, and their performance determined their values. There's ongoing work on transferring merchandise (like scarves or sweaters) into NFTs, enabling owners to register and verify the official merchandise as theirs.

6.8 NFT Use Case #8

Athlete's DNA Data

Professional athletes can use NFTs to store their personal medical information securely on the blockchain. Otherwise, this data could easily be leaked, and it can cost a lot of money when this happens. It can be a significant detriment if any sensitive data leaked in professional sports, from the business arrangement (selling/buying players, etc.) to tactical advantages through knowledge of their injuries. Any of these leaks can cost a match, a race, a season, or even a career.

6.9 NFT Use Case #9

People's Skills Or Time

This provides another monetization way for people by simply allowing them to issue tokenized ownership proofs of their skills or time, which can then be redeemed for their time or specific tasks. For example, people can publish NFTs for podcasts freelancing, videos, events, creating art, newsletters, charity, and many more.

6.10 NFT Use Case #10

Domain Names

Decentralized Domain Name services like **Ethereum Name Service (ENS)** and **Unstoppable domains** are getting the spotlight. ENS's users can exchange their address from a difficult-to-remember long string of numbers to "myname".eth, making it more user-friendly. Unstoppable Domains is powered by Crypto Name Service (CNS) and built on top of Ethereum Blockchain.

Your crypto address is like your Twitter or Instagram. Every name needs to be different and unique. If you have a very common name, there can be thousands of people wanting the same one. Twitter and Instagram don't allow users to sell their usernames, but ENS and Unstoppable domains do. You can buy and sell crypto addresses at your own will. The popular names are at a higher price compared to those less in demand.

Creating domain names is not complicated, but the difficulty lies in the domains' demand. So far, these two platforms have successfully proven in their attempt at decentralized domains built with the ERC-721 token standard.

6.11 NFT Use Case #11

Identification, Certification, and Licenses

NFTs hold unique information about certain goods or assets, making them useful for registration of identifications, certifications or licenses, and qualifications on the blockchain.

Traditionally, a course completion certificate or other licenses and degrees are usually awarded in either paper form or online copy. All the employers and universities that require these documents require copies of these to be attached as a reference before hiring someone in a company or institution. If such licenses or certifications cant be created as NFTs, it will save a lot of time and admins' efforts to check and verify those records. For these license- or certificate-holders, they will be able to store the evidence easier without worrying about losing it.

Actually, every human being has unique identifications, including personal profile, medical history, education, address, etc. NFTs can make these go digital, and you will find it is easier to control your data.

6.12 NFT Use Case #12

Supply Chain

Overall, Supply chain tracking is another strength of blockchain, and NFTs can play a significant role here. The compatibility comes when there's increased demand for efficient and transparent supply chain management techniques.

The Bigger Picture

The above are the most popular NFT use cases, though this is by no means an exhaustive list. The NFT potential is still generally and largely untapped, and possibilities are endless. As the industry continues to grow, NFT can potentially bloom new kinds of experiences.

Chapter 7

Other Ways to Generate Revenue From NFT

7.1 NFT Lending & Borrowing
7.1.1 Lending with Fungible assets Vs. Non-fungible ones

Crypto Lending platforms have experienced exponential growth during the past two years. Compared to the 2018 era when people were asking what would the future of the utility of the space, now we can see that lending is playing a significant role in providing real value in the markets for the products with real traction and adoption.

As the market continues to grow, it's natural for collectors to have the need to leverage their NFT assets without selling them, and the need can be stronger if you consider the intrinsic values. However, there are a few important differences when we compare lending with non-fungible and fungible assets:

1. With Fungile lending, the valuation is done automatically and precisely. The price is determined by the market objectively too. While in the NFT space, there's a big challenge for most projects since the price is not majorly driven by volume, instead of by scarcity. So the valuation can be subjective.

2. If we check the fungible assets lending platforms, they only operate with a handful of high-liquidity assets. But in the NFT space, this is almost impossible because there is not only a wide range of projects but inside every specific project, the properties vary a lot for each asset. It is the different property making them unique.

3. For fungible lending, the liquidation occurs automatically as the borrowing prices get closer to the market ones, increase the LTV ratio to the specific threshold. Thanks to this mechanism, the platforms and lenders will not lose in the entire process. But with NFT lending, we cannot have thresholds for verifying the whole project and the category of assets' actual volume associated with the collateral assets inside the game because the NFT market is driven by scarcity that will always have downtime or friction in the situation of automatic liquidating the assets by the system to cover the lenders' loss.

If we understand and consider these factors, we can see that NFT lending has some unique challenges compared to those traditional crypto lending with fungible ones. However, not all is lost.

7.1.2 Why we need NFT debt markets

In the NFT ecosystem, the debt market is a major missing piece. There's a need for people to both obtain loans from the NFTs and lease their NFTs. Many NFT users hold the assets in their wallets without using them unless they interact within the specific platform or play a particular game. When not in use, their NFTs sit in the wallet quietly and collect dust. It would be fantastic if there are platforms allowing users to put their assets to work by leasing them or using them as loan collateral. Also, it benefits other users who need their NFTs at that moment.

7.1.3 How the NFT collateralize loans work?

Let's look at how the platform **NFTfi** works to understand the process. NFTfi is a simple marketplace for NFT collateralized loans.

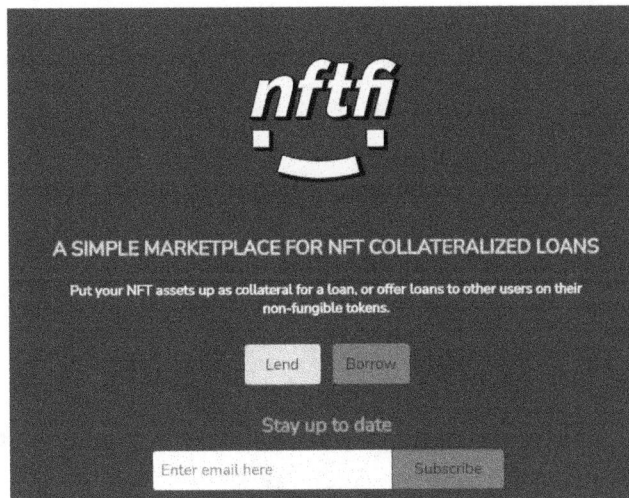

Fig 7.1 Nftfi

For Borrowers: Use your NFTs as the collateral. Borrowers can put any ERC-721 tokens for collateralization. Other users can offer them a loan. If borrowers accept the loan, the ETH gets paid out from the lenders' account to them, and the NFT will be locked in the NFTfi smart contract. Once they repay the loan, the assets will be transferred back to them. If they don't pay back the total repayment amount before the due date, their assets will be transferred to the lender.

For Lenders: Get attractive returns. Lenders can browse their favorite NFTs like Decentraland, cryoptoKitties to offer loans on assets they're happy to lend. Then submit the proposal, including the loan value, duration, and repayment values. In the worst case, the borrowers cannot pay, and they will get the asset. For them, small and short-term loans to others can provide them attractive returns too. But they need to understand the NFT assets they are offering and be willing to accept the collateral if the lender defaults.

7.1.4 NFT valuation questions

This is an interesting part. Let's say a CryptoKitty was sold for 30 ETH previously, but is it still value 30 ETH? <u>Etherscan</u> can help with this. We can see the what's the last sale price for this kitty. However, valuing an NFT at its previous sale price is straightforward but not accurate. A comparable analysis needs to be performed on the valuation regarding the kitty's species, properties, and the CryptoKitties' market trend as a whole.

To value the CryptoKitty accurately, we need either intimate knowledge of the CryptoKitties or an approach to a leading community member to ask for input. The most cost-effective price way may be leaving it to the markets.

7.1.5 An NFT valuation solutions

The NFT Collateralized loan marketplace could be an effective way to determine the NFTs' fair value. These marketplaces can allow users to post their NFTs as collateral, and other people can place bids on how much they are will to lend against them. The options of the loan term length and whether the lender offers DAI or ETH should be available too. This can make producing a fair valuation of NFTs possible.

For instance, after my own research, I am willing to lend 10 ETH with a five-month loan term. But another CryptoKitty expert knows this is a rare one and wants to offer 15 ETH for five months. The multiple offers and valuations can help produce a much more fair appraisement. It can be inefficient at the beginning but can eventually result in more solidified valuations on NFTs.

7.1.6 NFT lease

There could be an NFT leasing section in the marketplaces where users can browse different NFTs available to lease. The leasee can include the amount of them they're happy to have their NFTs be leased for, and the leaser can express the amount of them they want to have the asset. It would be effective for the markets to keep open to customization from both parties.

If users' behaviors can be determined, the market can focus on the popular categories, like "lend for one month" or "lend for one week." Having predefined and narrow lending categories can make it easy for new users to understand and help the leasing market grow from the original user base. This will offer another avenue for NFT owners to generate revenues.

Once NFTs go mainstream, the NFT leasing market size will be massive too. This is not only because people love trying new items and playing new games, but because people will want to put their assets into efficient use through leasing or lending them out.

7.1.7 How to value NFTs for lease

Like the NFT loan market, the NFT leasing market can help value the NFTs fairly: the leasing market can help settle on a fair leasing value for NFTs. It can be more dependant on the NFT types for the leasing market due to the assets' own nature.

For example, if you are breeding assets like Axies or CryptoKitties. They cannot always be bred efficiently. The leasing value for the activities like breeding can be high if the bred Axie or kitty has specific breeding properties. Other the other hand, if needs mine resources in CryptoSpaceCommanders urgently, you can lease a spaceship specifically for mining and then return the ship after the resources are obtained. This kind of need might be rare, hence theoretically speaking, the market would price this kind of asset cheap to lease.

Many factors need to be considered regarding the NFT leasing market values. However, the marketplaces can help discover the fair values for these activities.

7.1.8 Current state

A couple of solutions can currently provide NFT owners with choices to borrow funds by lending their NFTs as collateral: NFTfi, Starter, Lendroid, and UniLend. But most of them are still at the early stage. Among them, the Starter and NFTfi are two who went furthest. Starter has the Rinkeby version, and NFTfi is the only one on the mainnet.

So far, there seem to be no other solutions that work on NFT based lending actively. Two initiatives worth mentioned here:

At the beginning of 2020, a project called "Rocket" gained lots of publicity. Alex Masmej initiates it. While unfortunately, until writing the book, it hasn't been released to production yet. The team also wants to transfer the project's ownership to the highest bidder.

Another early-stage idea was from Dragos I. Musan. Dragos proposed theoretical solutions on how to use adequate Defi principles to bridge some of the current gaps in NFT markets. But so far, based on his listed ideas, only PoC solutions were developed, and it has similar functionalities as NFTfi.

7.1.9 Future of NFT Lending

We probably can see a considerable increase in market useability and activity by unleashing the Defi application power in the NFT space. NFT loan and leasing marketplaces will allow users to generate passive income, and more importantly, lead to a more accurate valuation of these NFT assets. Currently, we are at the Friendster-era of NFTs. However, we are getting closer to the MySpace-era by applying the traditional crypto market and modifying them for NFTs.

After NFTs reach millions of users and the highly liquid and robust marketplaces, we can see a Facebook-era with seamless user experience. Continuing building and adopting traditional crypto ecosystem use-cases for the NFT ecosystem will be the first step.

7.2 NFT Royalties

Since most NFTs are created as ERC-721 tokens, which means that after an artist initially sells their work to the buyer, that will be the only time they receive money for his/her work. If the buyer flips it on another secondary market later for ten times the price, the original artist sees none of that.

Right now, many platforms have realized this issue and are making efforts to improve this situation. Let's look at two platforms.

OpenSea

Users of Opensea now have the ability to earn revenues from secondary sales on items. Each time a piece is sold on OpenSea, the project owner can take a percentage of the sales as additional revenue. This not only allows creators to earn money from selling their initial work to users, but they can continue to earn as their game and marketplaces heat up.

Creators can just go to their storefront editor to set up the secondary sale fee. The revenue will be distributed every two weeks to the payment address specified by the creators. They can also contact OpenSea to change the frequency.

Zora

This is another new NFT platform allowing creators who make NFTs to set a "creator share" that is the percentage they will receive for future sales. For example, if they set the creator share is 20%. If the original piece was sold for 1 ETH, then someone sells that for 10 ETH later, the creator will receive an additional 2 ETH for that secondary sale. Since these creator shares are paid out automatically with the smart contracts and get auditable on Ethereum, the creator never needs to worry about tracking them down. They will just get paid in perpetuity to their original Ethereum address for creating the NFT.

Until now, you may have noticed a **problem**: currently, the methods these platforms are using for paying creator shares are not reproducible on the secondary market. The creator share percentages are only paid out if the secondary sale also happens on the same platform as the first sale- either OpenSea or Zora.

James Morgan and Zach Burks authored an "Ethereum Improvement

Proposal" (EPI-2981) to create the ERC-721 Royalty standard. The primary motivation of this is creating a modified NFT standard so that NFTs made, bought, or sold on one marketplace still pay out royalties no matter what the next market it will be sold on. This standard made it possible for creators to set the royalty amount paid to them on any marketplaces that implement these tokens.

With this concept, let's check back the Zora example. If the artists created the NFT on Zora, they would be entitled to their creator share if the buyers sell it on another marketplace. If more marketplaces will begin to adopt this standard, we could see another boom in the NFT ecosystem.

The NFT platform Recur has raised $5 million for perpetual cross-platform NFT royalties in March 2021, which is a promising step towards universal NFT royalties. Compared to the two platforms mentioned above, their main innovation is an ERC token standard allowing royalties to function regardless of platforms. "Our team is working in the process for Ethereum improvements, and our technology will be implemented at the layer of blockchain," said Recur Co-CEO Zach Bruch. "This new way can allow NFT created on RECUR's platform to move freely in the whole ecosystem while still can generate recurring royalties for the owners and IP holders. RECUR's ultimate goal is to make NFTs chain agnostic, keep NFTs and royalties decentralized."

An interesting example in Music Industry

Recently, a ConsenSys Mesh portfolio company, Treum, launched a project called EulerBeats, a 27 algorithmically generated music and art NFTs. When the number of prints in circulation grows for a particular original, the following print issuing price increases exponentially. ERC-1155, the modified ERC-721 version, was used. It means that for every future sale, the original LP holder can get 8% royalty, and Treum can also get 2% royalty. Within two weeks, this smart contract governing the unique LPs paid out 912 ETH that is $1,429,012 equivalent in royalties automatically.

For other NFTs whose metadata is hosted on the centralized web server, the music's metadata is included within the token implementation itself. This is critical since if the EulerBeats web got shut down, you still could run the beat and art generator script stored on the ETH chain in perpetuity.

We can store a verifiable unique audio piece on ETH, and future sales will be automatically paid out to the original owners. This can bring a new model for selling music.

It sounds cool. Enterprising artists have already begun to tokenize audio files and sell them directly to their fans as NFTs in 2021. At the same time, a more universal NFT royalty standard is coming out. But another new question comes out: **how does this all work with traditional performing rights organizations?**

The short answer is that what happens on ETH still exists within its ecosystem. Last year, ConsenSys and Harry Fox Agency were selected by the Mechanical Licensing Collective (MLC) to modernize music royalties' payment and data in the next few years. ConsenSys built the MLC portal in Jan, and this portal is evolving. More than 48 million songs and 9,400 music publishers are already included in the MLC portal. Also, they just inherited $424 million in unpaid royalties. As more PROs and music publishers begin to get comfortable with the benefits brought by NFTs, we will begin to see a convergence of these worlds in the near future.

Before then, if you are an artist and get disappointed with the current royalty system, it doesn't hurt to begin exploring what other musicians are doing in the NFT ecosystem.

Chapter 8

Other Options to Get Exposures to NFTs

As the NFT gain bull run, a question is repeatedly tweeted and commented on under NFT related posts:

"What is the best way to get exposure to NFT markets?"

It's almost impossible for every NFT investor to spend hours each day researching the ecosystem of NFTs. How to get exposure to NFT in the first place is still a hot question asked.

One of the problems with NFTs is that they are not the liquid tokens that are publicly traded, and you are able to buy when the hype train arrives. From the previous chapters, you probably learned that NFTs are super diverse, have many factors to drive their values, and are traded thinly. For newcomers, they cannot just simply jump and start buying. Well, they could, actually, but probably will regret it later since most of the NFTs are with little value.

So if you are not in the NFT ecosystem 24/7, how can you get exposure to NFT as investors? Let's explore some other options.

Options #1 – Ethereum (ETH)

Currently, 99% of NFT markets are priced in ETH. Other cryptocurrencies are beginning to gain traction as payment options, but ETH keeps dominant. Instead of check the USD equivalent, users will check the ETH price to make their NFT buying and selling decisions.

Let's say if you bought an NFT for 1 ETH when ETH is at $1500. Now they want to sell that NFT for 1.2 ETH. However, the value of ETH dropped to $1000, then that NFT would only be worth $1200 equivalent. Will you still sell it at this moment?

Currently, most of the NFT market participants would like to take the gain from ETH as they are long-term bullish about ETH, and they would likely reinvest that ETH into more NFTs. This may not always be the case, but I notice the majority of the NFT participants are trying to acquire more ETH.

Investing in ETH is a simple way to get exposure lightly to NFT markets: every NFT market participant uses ETH, and most of them reinvest their ETH into more NFTs.

Blockfi is a cryptocurrency platform that you can buy, sell, or exchange various cryptocurrencies, including ETH, at competitive prices. You can also start earning up to 8.6% APY the moment your trade is placed. Your interest accrues daily, and you will get paid monthly.

Options #2 -$RARI

Investing in $RARI token is another interesting approach to get exposure to NFTs as users to receive it for NFT trading. As we learned that Rarible is a big NFT exchange marketplace, and $RARI is their governance token.

$RARI immediately have incentivized people to start trading NFTs because they can earn $RARI by doing so. Users will not only earn a token from their NFT tradings but gain the ability to govern the Rarible platform. Since it's a governance token, you can use it to suggest and vote on new projects on the Rarible platform. Owning a token that can influence the major NFT exchange's decisions seems like an effective method to get NFT exposure.

$RARI is not a formal investing way and is better earned by active participation on Rarible. There are 75,000 tokens issued each week, with 50% reserved for sellers and 50% for buyers.

According to Rarible, only the following groups of people are eligible to participate in the airdrop:

Existing Rarible users: The active users can receive 2% of the total RARI supply based on the Liquidity Mining principle that is decided by the previous volume on Rarible.

NFT buyers/holders documented: 4% will be distributed among ETH addresses of all NFTs with documented sales on Dune Analytics.

Remaining NFT owners: Rarible knows that Dune Analytics may not hold all the data, so this is a correction for this issue. If you cannot find yourself on the list, but you know you have significant NFT holds, you can reach out to them for help.

Option #3 $WHALE

This is a relatively more direct way to get a connection to NFTs. $WHALE is a social token created by WhaleShark, a massive NFT collector. It's backed by the value of the NFTs held in something called "The Vault," which is a ~3,500 huge NFT collection that WhaleShark has acquired. As a $WHALE holder, you can use it to buy assets from the vault, including assets like virtual land, art, game assets, and many more.

Besides, nonfungible.com, an NFT data provider, offers monthly vault audits. Now, the WhaleShark controls the vault where NFTs can be purchased, but the whole $WHALE ecosystem moves to a DAO structure functioning as a vehicle for decision making.

Option #4 Flamingo DAO

Fig 8.1 Flamingo DAO

Flamingo DAO is an interesting NFT project launched by the people behind the successful DAO venture fund <u>LAO</u>. It's a for-profit DAO while focused on the NFT ecosystem specifically. Flamingo investing goes directly into NFTs, uses them as collateral for lending, fractionalizes NFTs, which goes deep into the whole NFT ecosystem.

One reason that can hold back people from it is they require a pricy minimum membership cost of 60 ETH. Also, they need US investors to be accredited.

Option #5 – NFT Bundles

One of the best ways for the majority of investors to gain exposure to NFTs is through the <u>Nifty Onez</u> NFT bundles constructed by GrowYourBase. These bundles exciting because <u>GrowYourBase</u> created them, which means they are filled with great NFTs. GrowYourBase is deeply involved in the NFT space and knows which NFTs to put into their bundles.

It's also an earn-and-learn platform, and you can get information on various NFTs as well as earn NFTs on their platform. The Onez bundles have many NFTs that can be fractionalized on another NFT fractionization platform- <u>NIFTEX</u>. Those fractions are called "shards," allowing users to purchase pieces of an NFT.

For instance, there are not many people who can afford to buy a $1,000,000 Banksy. However, the owner can fractionalize it on NIFTEX, and buyers can purchase shards of it, which allows them to have some percentage of ownership.

Two popular Onez bundles on NIFTEX:

Nifty ONEz Bundle: It's an art-focused bundle and includes art pieces from 20 leading crypto artists, such as Goldwead, Josie, Lucho Poletti, and Pranksy.

Meta Onez Virtual Land Bundle: Instead of art, it focused on virtual land. It contains 2 Decentraland lands, 2 Somnium Space lands, 21 Sandbox lands, and 5 Cryptovoxel parcels.

You can also see these two bundles on <u>shardmarketcap.io</u> website from Dapp Radar.

Fig 8.2 Shardmarketcap

These two choices may be ideal for people to get exposure to NFTs easily and the NFT space's specific sectors. If you are not sure which artists are hot, try a few Nifty ONEz shards. If you are not sure which virtual land exchange is the best, try some shards of Meta ONEz. As long as the curators designing these bundles understand what they are doing, this is an effective way for the public to get NFT exposure without spending an insane amount of time doing the NFT ecosystem research.

Chapter 9

NFT Risks and Scams & How to Avoid them

The NFT hype is real, and many popular ones have been sold for hundreds of dollars. While as exciting as the NFT space is, we need to pause and acknowledge risks too. As Garyvee tweeted,97-99% of NFT projects will be money losers, so learning and being patient are also important. We also need to consider and talk about the negatives.

9.1 NFT Major Trading Risks
1. Buying A Replica

In Feb 2020, it's reported that Fake Banksy nets over $1 million in ETH from the NFT sales. The account named "Pest Supply" had the branding and non-fungible tokens made in Banksy's signature graffiti-stencil style. Some users thought they got a great deal, and one tweeted, "I either just blew $750 or got the deal of lifetime on Banksy" But this person bought a fake Banksy because there is no authentic Banksy NFT on Rarible.

We need to stop and think are we getting the real deal? This is very similar to how traditional artworks. For example, if you have a Picasso that you feel is real, and everyone thinks it's real, it will be worth millions of dollars. However, what happens when you have a professional come in to verify, and they find out that it is not real. Instantly that painting becomes worth five dollars. The same thing is happening in the NFT world; people do fall victim to this scam, and it's likely will continue to happen. This account records showed hundreds of sales to buyers ranging from 0.116 Ethereum to over 60 Ethereum for a piece titled "NFT morons." If you don't want to be the morons, so what you have to do is to look into the NFT you're going to purchase, especially for those valuable ones.

It's not that hard. All you need to do is go to this piece and check its history: when it was sold, who placed the bid on it on all platforms. You may see that a fake account only has around 300 followers, but it's no way for the real Banksy account to have this small number of followers. Let's say if you're a Kingg's fan, you can also search this account in the search bar of the platform. If any other profiles show up, you can also double-check or cross-check on social media. Almost all of these people with reputations; they have a reputation for a reason. They are probably going to be on Instagram, Twitter, Facebook, or all over. If you check those people's social medial, you can probably find the link to their NFTs and bring you back to the same page you just found on the marketplaces. Now you can verify whether it's the real NFT accounts.

If you see something, and it looks to be too cheap and from a big artist, this is definitely a red flag. If you come across a person of influence selling an NFT for 15 ETH, pause for a second, go ahead, check the profile, the history, and cross-check with other social media.

2. Liquid Market

One of the biggest problems with the NFT market is that it is illiquid. When we look at the crypto markets, they are much more liquid, which means that when you buy crypto and things start going south, you can get out of your position or sell a quarter or all of it. However, in the NFT world, you cannot do that at the moment. It is an all-or-nothing sell. If we check crypto, it builds up support levels over time. For example, the bitcoin charts have moving averages, and we have a lot of data from the past to show us what range this crypto might be valued at. So even if it starts to decrease, we can slowly get out of our position. But in the NFT art or gaming world, the prices for these NFTs have no support level. They can go from $0 to $100,000 just overnight. One crypto punk sold for more than $700,000, but if we check its history, we can see that it was only sold twice: it was sold for about $2,000 and then sold for about $700,000. Between these sales, there were bids, and this is how it got to this high price.

It's critical to check the NFTs' value history. Is the NFT shot up overnight, or did it build value over time? It's risky because if you pay $1,000 or $5,000 on an NFT and its market goes south, and you can't just get out of your position. It is basically all or nothing under the illiquid market. When things go south, there are very few people that will want to buy your NFT that you paid thousands of dollars for. You might get nothing for that NFT. So every time when you are going to purchase the NFT, go and look through the history to check the previous sale prices, the bids, and the transfers.

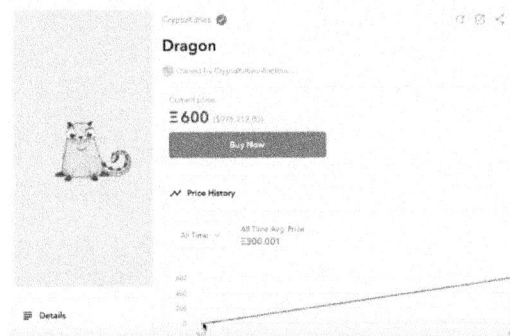

Fig 9.1 Example

Let's look at this CryptoKitty, it was sold for 0.002 ETH in 2018, and the next sale is 600 ETH in the same year, and we cannot any support level of the prices here. Also, its previous bids were mostly around 0.2 ETH. So whoever paid 600 ETH for this NFT is very likely to get stuck with it, and no one wants to buy it. Of course, it has the chance to be sold higher sometime in the future, but there's a lot of risks and little reward. We're risking putting money into an NFT that may not sell. So it's all about risk versus reward.

When it comes to the NFT world, whether it is NFT art or game, it's all about getting in early. It's a lot more difficult now because it's hard to predict which of these NFT collectibles and games will take off. It may be a little easier with NFT art since NFT art has a lot to do with reputation. When someone with a reputation sells NFT arts or collectibles, you already can predict that it likely will do well. For example, the Rick and Morty's creator, Justin Roiland, decided to sell NFTs on Nifty Gateway. In the beginning, his NFTs' prices were only hundreds of dollars. If you were able to get in early, these pieces are selling thousands of dollars.

It can still be risky when you're getting in early since you don't know if you're getting your hands on something valuable.

3. Wash Trades

This happens when someones create an NFT, lists it for sale, and then buys it back from themselves for a high price, creating the illusion that it is an NFT in demand. For example, if you see an NFT was sold for 500 ETH, but when you check the history and found it was just created five days ago and now it's sold for 500 ETH, this is very fishy. For the real ones, if you go through the trading history, and you will find that the real ones didn't just go from zero dollars to $1000 overnight. There are many offers along the way, and we'll see that it will bid up the price.

Also, if you ever see an account that is just having a ton of offers and sales from random addresses that no one can verify, it is likely a wash sale.

In summary, be very cautious when you're out there in this NFT world. When you are going to buy an NFT, make sure to check the history of the NFT and verify the creator.

9.2 NFT Scams You Must Avoid

1. Common Crypto Scams

If you fall for these NFT scams, you will lose everything that you worked so hard for. Imagine that you visit a MetaMask link you googled, and it turned out to be the phishing link; you will lose everything immediately you just put it into that fake wallet. A similar situation is even worse for NFT artists. In the NFT art world, you need to build a reputation, and your reputation is directly linked to your address. For example, on the first page of Rarible, you will see the top sellers over the last 30 days linked to their addresses. Let's say you built up a reputation, have been working very hard, and you made it to this top sellers list over the last 30 days. However, suddenly, your wallet has now been hacked, and you can no longer use that wallet. This is something that is very hard to rebuild unless you're someone who has a million followers. If you are someone like Mark Cuban, and your wallet was hacked. You can just go to Twitter and notify your followers that your wallet was hacked and put the new address link to your new wallet. But if you're an up-and-coming artist, or you're just new in the NFT space, you could have been working and grinding for over a year, building up a reputation. All of a sudden, the address you created, the reputation tied to your address, is at risk. You can no longer use that wallet, and it even gets worse. When it comes to NFT, you can set royalties, so if you create art and set a 10 or 20% royalty for every time that NFT is resold. Those royalties will go back to the wallet that created the NFT. So if you created a wallet, built up a reputation, sold NFTs, and you're getting royalties on those royalties that will go back to the original wallet. If your wallet is hacked or if you fell for this phishing scam, now someone has access to your wallet, and you can no longer use that. You have to move on.

This is only a fraction of what goes on in the crypto world. The crypto world is filled with scams. Wherever there is money, that is where scammers will go. The ecosystem of the crypto space is filled with money. There are also phishing links that can be sent to your email. You might get the scam from "Ledger" saying you're locked out of your wallet and asking you to provide your 12 words or 24 words seed phrase. Never share your seed phrases! Never! The only time you're ever going to use your seed phrases in crypto is when you initiate it. Remember that you are the one creating or restoring a ledger wallet or the other wallets. So when you get the email, it's probably a scam.

It also can be seen in exchanges, such as Coinbase. Fake emails actually look like they are from Coinbase, saying you have been locked out of your account, change your password, click this link go ahead. This is a phishing scam. So whenever you receive an email, you are not the one that initiated it; always be cautious. If you do ever get something from a site like Coinbase, maybe it is real, but the way you verify this is not by clicking the link you were sent, instead of entering the app the normal way you normally do. Do not respond to emails or links that you did not initiate.

2. Crypto Giveaway Scams

'Elon Musk' Crypto giveaway scams have stolen at least $587,000 from victims. This type is one of the most prevalent kinds of crypto scams and usually found on social medial platforms like Twitter and Youtube.

How do they work?

The hacker will impersonate or compromise a prominent company or public figure and claim to be giving away crypto. If you want to take part in these giveaways, you have to send an amount of crypto first to the address they advertise. They often promise to send back double, triple, or even more what you sent to them.

They want you to feel you are going to miss a huge opportunity if you don't do this. Usually, they specify the exact amount of crypto being given away, like "100,000 BTC giveaway." Then they will use fake accounts to comment and make it look like other people are receiving the cryptocurrencies. Their goal is to make you fear missing out and rush to send crypto to the scammers even before you consider carefully whether this giveaway is real or not.

Youtube and Twitter Giveaways

On Youtube, you may watch some live stream videos that a company or a celebrity is talking about something entirely unrelated to NFT and crypto. But there are full of bots in the comment section claiming they received a giveaway. You may even see some fake giveaway accounts have blue verified checkmarks on Twitter, making them look more legitimate. Some bots will reply to the tweets claiming the giveaways are real, and they just received. What they are doing is to create some "social proof" that the giveaways are legitimate.

Protecting Yourself

So far, almost all types of crypto or NFT giveaways are scams. There is a similar pattern that these fake giveaways follow: they pretend to be someone else and then ask you to send crypto before they give you more back. The best way to protect yourself is to educate yourself and gain the ability to identify this kind of scam.

Crypto transactions are irreversible, which means that you cannot get your money back. So once your crypto is sent to those fake giveaway addresses, it's gone forever. This is also the reason that this kind of scam is highly effective and keeps recurring.

The bottom line is that if anything sounds too good to be true, then it's very likely a scam. Think twice before you sent your crypto to others.

3. Youtube Impersonators

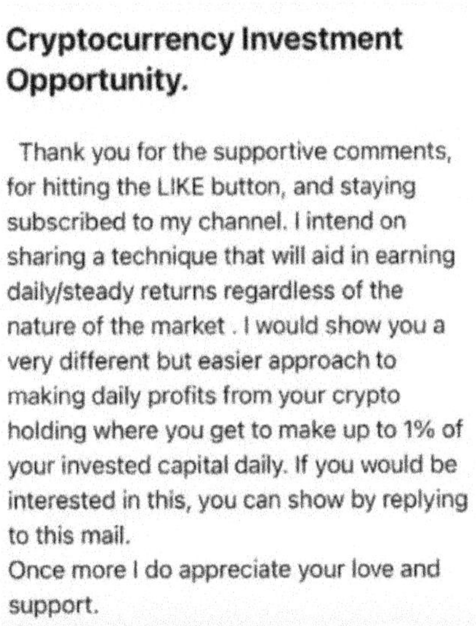

Cryptocurrency Investment Opportunity.

Thank you for the supportive comments, for hitting the LIKE button, and staying subscribed to my channel. I intend on sharing a technique that will aid in earning daily/steady returns regardless of the nature of the market . I would show you a very different but easier approach to making daily profits from your crypto holding where you get to make up to 1% of your invested capital daily. If you would be interested in this, you can show by replying to this mail.
Once more I do appreciate your love and support.

Fig 9.2 Message Example

You may receive some messages or emails like the above from some Youtubers, but actually, they are not from the Youtubers you like and follow. They look real, and very hard to tell what's fake or what's real. The way they speak can sound very genuine, and at the end, they'll say something like "reach out to me" or "send me money." However, these are scams too.

YouTubers usually cannot get access to the followers' emails. So make sure if you are not the one initiating, it is a scam. In the crypto space, always make sure you are the one that asks for the information first.

This kind of scam goes worse in the Youtube comments. There are many scammers and impersonators in the Youtube comments, trying to pretend that they're the Youtuber. They'll say things like "thank you for your comment, reach out to me on WhatsApp" or "here's my phone number." You will also see they spell Whatsapp in a funny way like "Wha-t-sapp" because Youtube will detect it. But when they write it in a funny way, Youtube doesn't really detect it. These scammers are flooding the comments, and people are actually responding to them and sending them money.

It is easy to tell which accounts are real or fake. If the creator of the video, there will be a gray area behind the name. If you see no gray area behind the name, this comment is not from the video's creator. You can also click on the profile, and it will show you how many subscribers there are. If you click on a scammer profile, you'll see there are zero or few subscribers.

Whenever someone asks you to contact them or ask you to send them money in crypto, you should always be the one initiating first.

Chapter 10

What's Next for NFTs?

The potential and possibilities for NFT are endless, and the recent record-breaking sales help push NFT technology forward. At the same time, there's a barrier to its mass adoption, which is lacking widespread education of the crypto world and blockchain technology. John G. Fields, the creator of Grow Your Base, said, "If you can educate people and allow them to get a taste of experience it, people then may not be intimidated by it."

Security is part of this education. The newcomers to the blockchain space need to understand how to keep their wallets and private keys safe so that their valuable digital assets won't be vulnerable to hackers. Due to their scarcity and rarity, many NFTs and digital investments can be very valuable. Losing them will lead to some headaches undoubtedly. To protect their values, digital assets' creators and developers must ensure that solid licensing and copyrighting are written into smart contracts. So far, the majority of the available crypto wallets are considerably difficult and complex for mainstream beginners and new users to onboard themselves. We can also see wallets that aim to improve this are being developed and released continuously, including <u>Enjin Wallet</u>, <u>Pillar wallet</u>, and <u>Wax Cloud Wallet</u>. Another wallet worth mentioning here is <u>NGRAVE ZERO</u>. It's designed to be the most secure and "coldest" crypto wallet that is seamless and user-friendly, allowing you to have peace of mind when interacting with your NFTs. Users can trade and store their digital assets in a protected and secure environment. <u>NGRAVE</u> also provides a high-quality touch screen and offers another interesting potential to enable owners to display their digital assets to others from a portable device.

The other aspect of educating the public needs to know how blockchain and NFTs are still very nerdy, technical, and even geeky. It's necessary to simplify this further to be easy to access and use for those who know nothing about these technologies. The Splinterlands's CEO, Dr.Jesse Reich, stated how the trouble "lies in making blockchain invisible to new users and still accessible to advanced users." Some NFT projects like CryptoKitties have introduced new users to blockchain successfully, and the recent rise and development of NFT use cases have fueled its adoption, but there is still a long way to go. Recently, the NFT excitement is concentrated in the niche areas of art, collectibles, and gaming. However, new NFT projects that merge continuously are slowly but expanding NFTs to other aspects of our physical lives for sure. Big brands are joining the fray too, for example, Nike has patented their shoes as NFTs and named "CryptoKicks" that allow users to breed different shoes to create a new custom sneaker. We probably will see how NFTs grow to become transferable between the physical and digital worlds. Yat Siu, the CEO of Animoca Brands, said, "If millions of people suddenly end up owning Nike virtual shoes, how many game companies may say, let's make use of those Nike shoes inside our digital games?"

When more and more people realize the value and potential that the NFTs can provide, an increasing number of major investors, big brands, and venture capital companies will be getting involved and take notice. It's reported that Jason Williams and Anthony Pmpliano, the co-founders of Morgan Creek Digital, made a "big bet" on digital art NFTs will surpass the physical art market.

We can also notice that the indie blockchain game developers have also started to successfully attract venture capital because of their ability to provide changed monetization models and incredibly long product life cycles, making them the ideal investments. The NFT sector's governance tokens are also sparking interest, similar to what they did for DeFi. There's no telling what exciting new ways DeFi and NFTs will discover to intermingle.

The NFT's future road can be with challenges and face regulatory hurdles. Regardless, the space of the crypto is still young and will continue to grow as an entire community with many more projects' production, even if the projects come, succeed, or fail.

Is the NFT phenomenon a bubble?

This is hard to say. Music and art themselves are challenging to value, and NFTs fall into this broad category. It could be a temporary mania that developed as a collective emotional reaction to the pandemic. Or it may just be the start point of a huge new virtual market segment.

For young risk-takers

The market of NFTs can be more efficient compared to the traditional ones. NFT is structured around virtual art marketplaces. If we consider the fees, they are below 5% or even 10% of the fees paid to traditional art brokers. The platforms like OpenSea and Rarible have counted tens of thousands of unique wallet connections every week.

The first group of cryptocurrency holders has turned into millionaires during this sector's impressive growth during the past five years. It is mostly the young risk-takers who like to experiment and can afford to become the crypto-wealthy generation. Actually, although there's extreme volatility of the price, studies have reported that the public is increasingly growing favorable cryptocurrencies' adoption. Their appetite for risk broadens the crypto-economy's possibilities.

There are already some very promising applications for the technology in the gaming and luxury industries that will reach maturity in the next three years gradually, but some would argue that NFT's craze will be short-lived, particularly in the art section.

The NFT market's audience is different from those involved in the traditional markets. It's the WallStreetBets's generation betting against those giant hedge funds, and Banksy's heirs destroyed the artwork. The NFT craze itself may be short-lived. However, more importantly, it could represent a big shift in where the virtual economy is headed. It is the first and foremost disruptive, for better or worse.

Conclusion

NFT is one of the favorite areas for investment in 2021. In the eye of the beholders, digital art is valuable, and NFTs make it possible to own one piece of this world. While many things still remain uncovered in the world of new NFTs. The original tweet of Jack Dorsey was sold for $2.5 million recently, which opened a new door for other similar transactions. The whole virtual world is getting the monetization that users have long dreamed of. The sale of in-game items has been long banned in auction sites, such as eBay, so the introduction of NFTs brings safer ways for gamers to sell their efforts to other people.

Now, hundreds of sites have claimed to produce authenticity certificates for everything in the physical artworks, too, from autographs to paintings. So even physical artworks are getting traded via NFTs. It's easier than ever to trade and authenticate these collectibles by securing all that on a single blockchain.

NFTs are a relatively new type of investment. Some have been sold for tens of millions of dollars, which proves that they're lucrative. While there is still a lot to learn about them. Besides, it can be challenging to put a fair price on digital art, making NFTs a risky investment.

So are NFTs the right investment for you? This book covers the basics of blockchain, cryptocurrency, and NFTs, as well as how to value, make, buy, sell, trade, and invest NFTs. If you decided to invest in NFTs, set your spending limit and only buy what you can afford to lose. As mentioned, NFTs are highly speculative, so it's unrealistic to expect to get rich as soon as you go into it. In addition, It can be a good idea to keep the majority of your money in other safer investments like ETFs and funds. Since if a bulk of your portfolio is invested in relatively safe places, you will be in a better position to take on the risky investments.

Investors should expect digital art masterpieces' prices to rise since NFTs help collectors validate ownership, lowering the risk of piracy and fraud. Also, don't be surprised when the price of real-world collectibles increases. At the same time, beware of the unexpected risks. For Jack Dorsey's iconic original tweet, it could go up in value, but many other NFTs fizzle out before the public can understand what things are worth.

NFTs are an interesting new kind of investment, but they're not suitable for everyone. If you are curious about NFTs and have available cash to spare, it may not hurt to get your feet wet. Otherwise, it's better to observe this phenomenon unfold from the sidelines where your money can be kept safer.

As always, be cautious of how you invest. It can be a good time to be in NFTs but do not put more money in than you can afford to lose.

References

1. CONWAY, L. (2020, October 17). Blockchain Explained.

   Investopedia.

   https://www.investopedia.com/terms/b/blockchain.asp

2. What Is Blockchain Technology? How Does It Work? | Built In.

   (2020). BUILTIN. https://builtin.com/blockchain

3. Kulkarni, A. (2018, November 29). Blockchain Vs. Cryptocurrency:

   How The Two Relate To Each Other. Medium.

   https://medium.datadriveninvestor.com/blockchain-vs-

   cryptocurrency-how-the-two-relate-to-each-other-edf7632fe9de

4. Understanding The Different Types of Cryptocurrency. (2021,

   January 15). Sofi.

   https://www.sofi.com/learn/content/understanding-the-

   different-types-of-cryptocurrency/

5. What are the Popular Types of Cryptocurrencies? (2021, March

   9). Equity Trust. https://www.trustetc.com/blog/types-of-

   cryptocurrency-explained/

6. W, O. (2020, November 13). What is NFT? - Cortex Labs. Medium.

   https://medium.com/cortexlabs/what-is-NFT-da442a7d2728

7. Thaddeus-Johns, J. (2021, March 12). What Are NFTs, Anyway?

   One Just Sold for $69 Million. The New York Times.

https://www.nytimes.com/2021/03/11/arts/design/what-is-an-nft.html

8. Steinwold, A. (2019, October 8). The History of Non-Fungible Tokens (NFTs) - Andrew Steinwold. Medium. https://medium.com/@Andrew.Steinwold/the-history-of-non-fungible-tokens-nfts-f362ca57ae10

9. Brown, A. (2021, March 4). What Is An NFT—And Should You Buy One? Forbes. https://www.forbes.com/sites/abrambrown/2021/02/26/what-is-an-nft-and-should-you-buy-one/?sh=1709e87824b2

10. Chang, H. (2020, March 25). Understanding the value of Non-Fungible Tokens (NFT). Medium. https://medium.com/@changhugo/understanding-the-value-of-non-fungible-tokens-nft-49d2713bdfc4#:%7E:text=NFTs%20are%20interesting%20because

11. Crockett, Z. (2021, March 7). Why NFTs are suddenly selling for millions of dollars. The Hustle. https://thehustle.co/why-nfts-are-suddenly-selling-for-millions-of-dollars/

12. Wallet, S. I. (2020, August 5). What is the Best Wallet for DeFi? - SelfKey Decentralized Finance. SelfKey. https://selfkey.org/what-

is-the-best-wallet-for-defi/

13. Money, R. (2020, November 12). 7 Best DeFi Wallets (Updated 2020) - Rekt Money. Medium. https://rektmoney.medium.com/7-best-defi-wallets-updated-2020-f9a8ec0ea57b

14. Carter, W. (n.d.). Enjin Wallet: Detailed Review and Full Guide on How to Use It. Wallets.Com. https://wallets.com/enjin-review/

15. Spalter, A. (2021, February 26). Anne Spalter: I'm an Artist. Should I Make an NFT? CoinDesk. https://www.coindesk.com/im-an-artist-should-i-make-an-nft

16. Martin, R. (2021, March 15). How to Create and Sell Your First NFT. Kapwing Resources. https://www.kapwing.com/resources/how-to-create-and-sell-nft-crypto-art/

17. Atallah, A. (2021, March 19). Create NFTs for Free on OpenSea. OpenSea Blog. https://opensea.io/blog/announcements/introducing-the-collection-manager/

18. Marketplace, Z. O. M. —. N. G. N. (2021, January 21). Gas fees suck — mint NFTs without a transaction on Mintable! Medium. https://mintable.medium.com/gas-fees-suck-mint-nfts-without-

a-transaction-on-mintable-8d54b85a471c

19. Guadamuz, A. (2021, March 17). Copyfraud and copyright infringement in NFTs. TechnoLlama. https://www.technollama.co.uk/copyrfraud-and-copyright-infringement-in-nfts

20. Bailey, J. (2021, March 16). NFTs and Copyright. Plagiarism Today. https://www.plagiarismtoday.com/2021/03/16/nfts-and-copyright/

21. Walker, C. (2021, March 19). 4 Best Platforms to Create Your NFT On •. Benzinga. https://www.benzinga.com/money/best-platforms-to-create-your-nft-on/

22. Journal, T. W. S. (2021, March 13). Want to buy an NFT? Here's what to know. Fox Business. https://www.foxbusiness.com/money/want-to-buy-nft-what-to-know

23. How To Buy NFTs. (2021, March 8). [Video]. YouTube. https://www.youtube.com/watch?v=MXnLUpZBi4A

24. The Bitcoin Express. (2021, February 18). 3 Methods To Find Valuable NFTs. YouTube. https://www.youtube.com/watch?v=ETu9VluW0XQ

25. NFT Tutorial: How To Buy, Sell, And Interact With Non-Fungible

Tokens. (2020, October 9). [Video]. YouTube. https://www.youtube.com/watch?v=EF3zWvxGm4M

26. How to Sell NFTs after Minting. (2021, March 14). [Video]. YouTube. https://www.youtube.com/watch?v=4Eub6sJf9A4

27. Peaster, W. M. (2021, March 16). How to value NFTs. Bankless. https://newsletter.banklesshq.com/p/how-to-value-nfts

28. Guides. (n.d.). NFT20 Docs. https://docs.nft20.io/guides/

29. Nifty, V. (2021, January 16). Introducing NFT20 V0.1 - Very Nifty. Medium. https://verynifty.medium.com/introducing-nft20-v0-1-731002094d7a

30. Kaya, S. (2020, July 31). How to Use BoxSwap to Swap Crypto Collectibles (NFTs). Dappgrid. https://dappgrid.com/boxswap-swapping-crypto-collectibles-nfts/

31. Y. (2019, March 19). Swapping NFT's with BoxSwap in the evolving dApp gaming industry. Medium. https://the-ycb.medium.com/swapping-nfts-with-boxswap-in-the-evolving-dapp-gaming-industry-f06f98f83fd5

32. Schroeder, S. (2021, March 17). Crypto wallet MetaMask now lets you swap tokens on your phone. Mashable. https://mashable.com/article/metamask-swaps/?europe=true

33. NFT Trading | What Are NFTs & How To Get Started.

Daytrading.Com. https://www.daytrading.com/nft

34. Merre, R. (2021, March 14). The big five NFT use cases. CryptoSlate. https://cryptoslate.com/the-big-five-nft-use-cases/

35. Moore, J. (2020, November 23). Non-fungible Token Use Cases Across Industries. PayBito. https://www.paybito.com/non-fungible-token-use-cases-across-industries/

36. Zafar, T. (2021, January 28). Top 5 NFT Use Cases. CryptoTicker. https://cryptoticker.io/en/top-5-nft-use-cases/

37. Minddeft Marketing. (2020, December 10). NFTs and their Use-Cases: The Minddeft Guide. MindDeft Technologies Blog. https://minddeft.com/blog/nfts-and-their-use-cases-the-minddeft-guide/

38. Definition and Use Cases of Non-Fungible Tokens (NFT). (2020, August 24). Ivanontech. https://academy.ivanontech.com/blog/definition-and-use-cases-of-non-fungible-tokens-nft

39. Ngetich, D. (2020, September 11). ETHwriter: Exploring Underexplored NFT Use Cases - Dalmas Ngetich. Voice. https://www.voice.com/post/@dalmas254/ethwriter-exploring-underexplored-nft-use-cases-1599839659-1

40. S. (2021, January 30). What The Future Holds for NFT Lending — Making The Case for Fast Loans and Pool Lending. Hacker Noon. https://hackernoon.com/what-the-future-holds-for-nft-lending-making-the-case-for-fast-loans-and-pool-lending-xzo3295

41. Novitović, M. (2021, March 11). NFT Lending – Current State and What's Next? MVP Workshop. https://mvpworkshop.co/blog/nft-lending-current-state-and-whats-next/

42. Steinwold, A. (2019a, August 26). NFT Valuation, Lending & Borrowing: Putting Non-Fungible Assets to Work. Medium. https://medium.com/@Andrew.Steinwold/nft-valuation-lending-borrowing-putting-non-fungible-assets-to-work-ce92c61bad50

43. Thurman, A. (2021, March 27). Recur raises $5 million for perpetual cross-platform NFT royalties. Cointelegraph. https://cointelegraph.com/news/recur-raises-5-million-for-perpetual-cross-platform-nft-royalties

44. Can NFTs Crack Royalties And Give More Value To Artists? (2021, March 2). ConsenSys. https://consensys.net/blog/blockchain-explained/can-nfts-crack-royalties-and-give-more-value-to-artists/

45. Steinwold, A. (2020, November 13). 😎 ☑ 💎 How To Easily Get

NonFungible Token (NFT) Market Exposure. Medium.
https://medium.com/@Andrew.Steinwold/how-to-easily-get-nonfungible-token-nft-market-exposure-47a88334dc78

46. 3 Major NFT Trading Risks. (2021, February 25). [Video]. YouTube.
https://www.youtube.com/watch?v=JkOu2_oeWyU

47. NFT ART SCAM YOU MUST AVOID!! (2021, March 15). [Video].
YouTube. https://www.youtube.com/watch?v=aQ9dOl1WiEw

48. Security check. (n.d.). Kraken. https://support.kraken.com/hc/en-us/articles/360057159411-Beware-of-crypto-giveaway-scams-

49. Why 2021 Will be the Year of Non-Fungible Tokens (NFTs). (2021,
January 6). Linkedin. https://www.linkedin.com/pulse/why-2021-year-non-fungible-tokens-nfts-ruben

50. Datta, D. (2021, March 21). Is the NFT phenomenon a bubble? Or
a new beginning? Rediff.
https://www.rediff.com/business/special/is-the-nft-phenomenon-a-bubble-or-a-new-beginning/20210321.htm

51. Brockman, K. U. T. (2021, March 26). There's no limit to how
much a meme costs: Should you invest in NFTs right now? The
Motley Fool.
https://eu.usatoday.com/story/money/investing/2021/03/26/sho

you-invest-in-nfts-right-now/43480051/

52. Yeung, T. (2021, March 10). What are NFTs? An Investor's Guide to Investing in Non-Fungible Tokens. InvestorPlace. https://investorplace.com/what-are-nfts-an-investors-guide/

Fig 1.1 Pepe the Frog. (n.d.). [Illustration]. Wikipedia. https://en.wikipedia.org/wiki/Pepe_the_Frog

Fig 1.2 cryptopunks. (n.d.). [Illustrations]. https://www.larvalabs.com/cryptopunks

Fig 1.3 CryptoKitties. (n.d.). [Illustration]. https://www.cryptokitties.co/

Fig 1.4 Non-Fungible Token Ecosystem. (2019). [Graph]. https://www.theblockcrypto.com/2019/02/08/mapping-out-the-non-fungible-token-ecosystem